India-Central Asia Economic Relations:
Prospects and Challenges

India-Central Asia Economic Relations:
Prospects and Challenges

Ishfaq Ahmad Malik

PARTRIDGE
A Penguin Random House Company

To order additional copies of this book, contact
Partridge India
000 800 10062 62
orders.india@partridgepublishing.com

www.partridgepublishing.com/india

Affectionately Dedicated to

My Respected Family Members
And
Urwah, Sairah & Ehsan

CONTENTS

LIST OF TABLES

LIST OF FIGURES

PREFACE

Historically India and Central Asian republics have strong relations. In the ancient times both regions were powerful centres with great deal of economic and cultural relations. The ancients "Silk Route" connects India and Central Asian region due to which both have experienced the exchanges in cultural, political and economic spheres. However, during Soviet period economic relation between India and Central Asia were under control of Moscow. But after collapse of Soviet Union these republics tries to develop their economic and political relations with other economies.

In the current global economic scenario this age-old relationship has attained greater significance. Despite the fact that the present relationship between India and CAR's is increasing but below than expected potential level. The value of merchandise trade between two regions increased from US$ 114.05 million in 2000-01 to US$746.32 million in 2012-13. The significant increase in the total trade was mainly due to the development of diplomatic relation and signing many agreements. Similarly, the commercial relation between the two regions is on progress. Central Asia is emerging as potential destination for India's overseas investment. Number of Indian companies has set up wholly owned and joint ventures in the CAR's in different sectors like oil and gas, pharmaceuticals, information technology, food products and petroleum products. In this respect, for the facilitation of trade and investment, India has created an institutional framework and set up working groups in various field. Moreover, this region has great significance for India in energy sector. The economic development of India is very much depending upon the development of energy, the growth of economy causes an increase in the demand for energy as well. In India, the domestic consumption of energy is more than domestic production. This imbalance in demand and supply creates a problem for the growth of the growing economy. It is well reflected by the fact that India is the world's 11th energy producer while being the world's sixth largest consumer in the global energy market. Due to growing energy demand in India, she is trying to deepening its energy trade relationship with other countries, such as energy rich region the Persian Gulf and Central Asia. Currently India is importing oil from Gulf countries, Africa and other Middle East countries. But the geopolitical volatility in Middle East especially Libya and Egypt affects negatively on crude oil production in the region, as a result oil prices rise, which stimulates inflation in India. This instability creates apprehension in the minds of Indian policy planners to diversify its import sources of energy like Central Asian republics which offers an opportunity in this regard. Therefore, India has opportunity to look towards CAR's which is best alternative for India. This region is holding large energy resources while as India has the potential and capacity to enhance its participation and presence in the various sectors in the said region.

India has difficult task ahead before it can successfully exploit these opportunities with CAR's. Though India and CAR's have age-old relationship and with the signing of trade agreements, and MoU's since 1996, much of the problems seem to have been resolved. Still there remains number of challenges, which are difficult to be resolved and could not be isolated from the social, political, ideological and economic factors of these nations. Looking at the current trade level between these two regions, the trend is not in desired direction.

I wish that this book would be helpful to government and non-government organisations, academicians, policy makers and scholars of the two regions to work towards strengthening and improving their economic ties.

Srinagar, May 2014 Ishfaq Ahmad Malik

ACKNOWLEDGEMENTS

My sincere gratitude to the charismatic personality, Dr. Mohd. Afzal Mir, whose invaluable guidance, strong motivation, encouragement and support made it possible to complete this book. I am indebted to Dr. Gulshan Sachdeva, JNU, Delhi, Dr. Meena Singh Roy, IDSA, New Delhi, and Dr. Ram Upendra Das, RIS New Delhi for their help extended during the course of my study. Moreover, it gives me lot of pleasure to put here the names of research colleague, Mr. Mohd. Aslam Bhat, and I express my sincere thanks to all my close friends for their constant support and encouragement, particularly Mr. Ajaz Ahmad Rather and his wife, further special thanks goes to Mr. Mohd. Idrees Malik, Mr. Arshid Habib and Mr. Sameer Ahmad.

Ishfaq Ahmad Malik

GLOSSARY OF WORDS

ADB	Asian Development Bank
APK	Assembly of Peoples of Kazakhstan
BCF	Billion Cubic Feet
BCM	Billion cubic meters (of natural gas)
BP	British Petroleum
BTC	Baku–Tbilisi–Ceyhan Pipeline
CAR's	Central Asian Republics
CEC	Central Electoral Commission
CES	Common Economic Space
CICA	Conference on Interaction and Confidence-Building Measures in Asia
CIS	Commonwealth of Independent States
CITIC	China International Trust and Investment Corporation
CNPC	China National Petroleum Company
CPC	Caspian Pipeline Consortium
CPSU	Communist Party of the Soviet Union
CSTO	Collective Security Treaty Organization

DVK	Democratic Choice of Kazakhstan (*Demokraticheskiy Vybor Kazakhstana*)
EEU	Eurasian Economic Union
EIA	Energy Information Administration
EITI	Extractive Industry Transparency Initiative
EPW	Economic and Political Weekly
EPZ's	Export Processing Zones
EurAsEC	Eurasian Economic Community
EXIM	Export Import Bank
FCPA	Foreign Corrupt Practices Act
FDI	Foreign Direct Investment
FEMA	Foreign Exchange Management Act
FERA	Foreign Exchange Regulation Act
FTP	Foreign Trade Policy
GDP	Gross National Product
GNI	Gross National Income
GOI	Government of India
HDI	Human Development Index
IEF	Index of Economic Freedom
IMF	International Monetary Fund
IOC	International Oil Company
IPI	Iran-Pakistan-India Gas Pipeline
IT	Information Technology
KBTU	Kazakh-British Technical University

KCTS Kazakhstan Caspian Transportation System

KEGOC Kazakhstan Electricity Grid Operating Company

KIMEP Kazakhstan Institute of Management, Economics and Forecasting

KSNU Kazakh State National University

MEMR Ministry of Energy and Mineral Resources

MGIMO Moscow State Institute of International Relations

MoU Memorandum of Understanding

MTOE Million Tons Oil Equivalent

NEER Nominal Effective Exchange Rate

NEP New Economic Policy

NFRK National Fund for the Republic of Kazakhstan

NIOC National Iranian Oil Company

NOC National Oil Company

ODIHR Office for Democratic Institutions and Human Rights

OSCE Organization for Security and Cooperation in Europe

PPCK Party People's Congress of Kazakhstan

PSA Production Sharing Agreement

RAOEES Russian Unified Energy Systems

RBI Reserve Bank of India

SAARC South Asian Association for Regional Cooperation

SCO Shanghai Cooperation Organization

SME Small- and Medium-scale Enterprise

SPECA Special Program for the Economies of Central Asia

SWG	Special Working Group
TAPI	Turkmenistan-Afghanistan-Pakistan-India Gas Pipeline
TCF	Trillion Cubic Feet
TCF	Trillion Cubic Feet
TCP-gas	Trans-Caspian Pipeline - Gas
TCP-oil	Trans-Caspian Pipeline - Oil
TDR	Trade Development Report
TOT	Terms of Trade
TST	Thousand Short Tones
UDP	United Democratic Party of Kazakhstan
UNCTAD	United Nations Conference on Trade and Development
UNDP	United Nations Development Program
UNECE	United Nations Economic Commission for Europe
UNESCAP	United Nations Economic and Social Commission for Asia and the Pacific
UPUK	Union of People's Unity of Kazakhstan
USSR	Union of Soviet Socialist Republics
WDR	World Development Report
WTO	World Trade Organization

CHAPTER 1

Economic Performance of India and Central Asia

Economic interdependence of individuals in a society and between societies is as old as humanity itself. While this interdependence around the globe integrated overtime trade, finance and people, contemporary growth of technology, and population have spread the horizons beyond expected spheres with the added dimensions and importance. Specifically, towards the end of the 20ᵗʰ century, the thrust on globalization by leading international economic organizations like IMF, World Bank, World Trade Organization, etc. made economic isolation of countries impossible. The existence of economic interdependence and economic relations between countries is based, on principle, on the possibility and emergence of mutual gain that trade creates for goods with difference in valuation across regions and markets. Basis of the economic interdependence is the possibility of gains that countries share between themselves.

In recent times, such an international sharing has intensified and has further stretched the economic interactions across the globe. The free flow of capital and advanced technology stimulates trade of goods and services. Markets have extended their reach around the world, in the process creating new linkages among national economies. At times, functioning of such linkages has been referred to as globalization—a phenomenon quite popular both in popular and academic literature. Nonetheless looking into the economic

1

interpretations of the term globalization, it refers to the process of resource—capital, labour, technology, raw material—and product mobilization across nations and the emergence, and flourishing of the institutions and techniques as well as infrastructure that support such vast quantum of mobilization.

The phenomenon, by reframing the positions of individuals, groups and nation states as well as the emergent "global community" leads to redefining of consideration—almost in all the different ways that concern individual and collective existence—at all the tires of involvement. Despite the fact, globalization has its economic and other "bads" for irresistibly globalizing pockets of the world, countries, in general, find it advantageous to forge economic ties with other nations.

Well-managed economic relations have the potential to accelerate the process of economic development. International trade provides opportunities to different business and production sectors to access markets much larger than the domestic ones. Consequently, more competitive firms and farms have advantage to expand their output. Economic relations provide the urge to develop the knowledge and experience that make development possible and furnish the means to accomplish it.

Commodity specialization, as exhibited and emphasized by classical and modern theories on international trade, like Ricardo and Heckscher-Ohlin, plays a major role in increasing production due to specialization. Specialization in the area of comparative cost advantage leads to overall international efficiency in resource utilization pushing up overall production as well as global consumption. Many scholarly works (Kruger, 1975; Balassa, 1978; Bhagawati, 1982; Srinivasan, 1985; Williamson, 1978; Awokuse, 2003) focus on theoretical and empirical relation between degree of openness and growth rates of countries. In principle, given rules are fair enough, openness facilitates better resource allocation, decreases average cost and increases production efficiency.

Similarly, investment in the export sector, and growth of economy are directly proportional, thus output increases (Rana and Dowling, 1990). However, Vernon (2006) views opposite: growth of exports is dependent on economic growth with innovation in technology, which leads to competition. The strategy of East Asian countries before 1970's is an example in this respect. These countries adopted an inward strategy policy, self-reliance and number of public sector undertakings. These policies were the cause for rent seeking activities and misallocation of resources (Bhagawati, 1982; Srinivasan, 1985). Nevertheless, on adopting an export oriented economic strategy, these countries could maintain sustainable level of growth and fulfil all the basic objectives for the welfare of the economy.

Romer's (1986) and Lucas's (1988) endogenous growth theory provide a theoretical base for proportional relation between long-term economic growth and international trade and development. The endogenous theory postulates inverse relation relationship between trade restrictions and rate of economic growth and development. This theory focused on international trade flow research and development, economies of scale, increasing specialization, and availability of new goods and services in the market. The empirical study of Edwards (1993) and Pack (1994) also shows that openness leads to faster growth. For example, the estimation of time-series and cross-section studies show that if real GDP increases by 0.2 percent, international trade increases by 1 percent (Van den Berg and Lewer, 2006). Equally Waczing and Welch's (2008) empirical study suggests that, countries that open their economy faces annual growth rate at about 1.5 percent higher than before liberalization. Therefore, a strategy for enhanced economic relations among countries aims at the increasing economic growth and industrialization. Reaping benefits from the foreign sector, being an integral part of an economy therefore, calls for an integrated approach involving strengthening of institutions and infrastructure—facilitating economic relations—as well as coordinated involvement of the different sectors. Thus, the fields of production, trade as well as finance have to develop in order to support each other.

The most important fundamental and enduring component of economic relations is trade. The trade of goods and services help the participating countries to reap benefits by exporting goods and services, which are produced at comparatively lower cost, and importing those having a comparatively higher cost in comparison to the trading partner(s). Thus trade brings down cost of availability of those goods and services for which there is comparative disadvantage in an economy. Different countries use different means to foster bilateral trade. Regulatory relaxations along with relaxations in imports excise and customs play an important role in fostering of bilateral trade.

Another important aspect of bilateral economic relations is the investment made in each other's country. Inflow of investment has proved to be beneficial for many developing economies in their speedy economic transformation. Many countries across the globe have undertaken liberalization policies to attract foreign investment into their economy. Apart from the other advantages that the investors, particularly from the developed countries, may reap, cheap raw material and labour costs provides them the necessary incentive to move their capital out from their own economies. Thus, they invest in countries with likely higher returns for their capital. Until now, foreign direct investment (FDI) is considered preferred type of capital inflows.

Good bilateral economic relations also help countries to get loans and economic aid from other countries during times of need. This is especially beneficial for developing and less developed countries. These relations may play a strategic role in the growth and development of an economy. One of the more important advantages for the developing nations from bilateral economic relations is the employment generation. With the growth of trade and inflow of capital to these countries, economic activity is boosted resulting in the growth of the economy and generation of more employment opportunities. Harmonious economic ties may also help people finding jobs in other countries.

The prospects of higher growth and industrialization has driven economies in the last half of the 20th century, particularly the concluding decades to integrate with other economies at an accelerated pace. Countries vie in all respects of this integration to benefits more from opportunities thrown up by what is famously known as globalization. A statistical portrayal of this trend depicts the approach of modern economies towards greater economic engagements with other countries and partially substantiates the belief that trade enhances the possibilities of growth.

The world merchandise trade by region and selected economies is shown in table 1.1. It shows that world's top importers and exporters are the largest industrial countries. The world's value of merchandise trade in 2011 was US$ billion 17779, with the China US$ billion 1899, followed by USA US$ billion 1481. China is growing rapidly in terms of the world's largest merchandise exporter surpassing the USA and other growing Asian economies. As far as the CIS countries are concerned, they export US$ billion 788, in which Russia individually exports US$ billion 522, more than two-third of total CIS countries exports. The data reveals small share of exports of both CIS countries and India as well.

Table 1.1: World Merchandise Trade by Region and Selected Economies, 2011 (US$ billion and Percentage)

	Exports				Imports			
	Value	Annual Percentage Change			Value	Annual Percentage Change		
	2011	2005-11	2009	2010	2011	2011	2005-11	2009	2010	2011
World	17,779	10	-23	22	20	18,000	9	-23	21	19
North America	2.283	8	-21	23	16	3,090	5	-25	23	15
United States	1,481	9	-18	21	16	2,265	5	-26	23	15
Canada	452	4	-31	23	17	462	6	-21	22	15
Mexico	350	9	-21	30	17	361	8	-24	28	16
South& Central America	749	13	-23	26	27	727	16	-25	30	24
Brazil	256	14	-23	32	27	237	20	-27	43	24
Other South and Central America	493	12	-24	22	27	490	14	-25	24	25
Europe	6,601	7	-22	12	17	6,854	7	-25	13	17
European Union (27)	6,029	7	-22	12	17	6,241	7	-25	13	16
Germany	1474	7	-23	12	17	1254	8	-22	14	19
France	597	4	-21	8	14	715	6	-22	9	17
Netherlands	660	8	-22	15	15	597	9	-24	17	16
United Kingdom	473	4	-23	15	17	636	4	-24	16	13
Italy	523	6	-25	10	17	557	6	-26	17	14
CIS	788	15	-36	31	34	540	17	-34	30	30
Russian Federation	522	14	-36	32	30	323	17	-34	30	30
Africa	597	11	-30	29	17	555	14	-15	15	18
South Africa	97	11	-24	31	20	122	12	-27	27	29
Middle East	1228	15	-31	27	37	665	12	-15	13	16
Asia	**5534**	**12**	**-18**	**31**	**18**	**5568**	**13**	**-20**	**33**	**23**
China	1899	16	-16	31	20	1743	18	-11	39	25
Japan	823	6	-26	33	7	854	9	-28	26	23
India	297	20	-15	33	35	451	21	-20	36	29

Source: *WTO Secretariat*

Moreover, there are other examples from other regions of the world, which firmly confirm that export oriented economic strategy leads to growth in the overall economic strength of countries. Table 1.2 shows the average growth rate of real GDP and trade in the High Performance Asian Economies (HPAEs). These include Hongkong, Singapore, Korea and Taiwan (Asian Tigers) and Malaysia, Indonesia, Thailand and China. The table shows that real GDP grew at the average rate of 8.1 percent in the HPAE's during the 2010 and 4.4 in 2011. During the same years growth rate of real GDP in China was 10.4 percent and 9.9 percent respectively. However, average growth rate of exports in these countries was higher than real GDP, which stands 14.9 in 2010.

Table 1.2: Average Growth of Real GDP and Trade in HPAE's, 2010 and 2011

	Growth of Real GDP		Growth of Exports	
	2010	2011	2010	2011
Korea	6.2	3.8	14.5	9.1
Hong Kong	7.0	4.7	16.8	4.9
Singapore	14.5	4.8	19.2	4.0
Thailand	7.8	2.0	14.2	8.8
Indonesia	6.1	6.5	14.9	15.9
Malaysia	7.2	4.8	9.9	4.4
Average	**8.1**	**4.4**	**14.9**	**7.8**
China	10.4	9.9	28.4	11.3

Source: *World Bank, World Development Report, 2012*

Table 1.2 reveals data from world to East Asian Economies show that outward-oriented strategy retains a favourable effect to performance of growth. Additionally, it provides an extension of market, specialization in production and positive external economies with a reduction in unemployment, inflation rate and poverty. Indeed, the major factors contributing to the high growth rate of exports in these economies were high rate of saving and investment, adoption of new technology and shift from agrarian to industrial economies.

Fig. 1.1:   World Output and Export

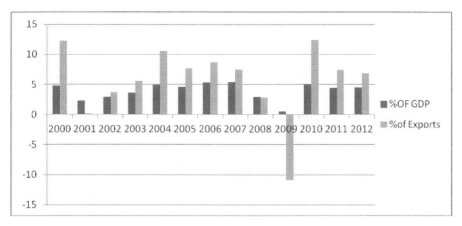

Source: *World Bank, World Development Report, 2012*

In the past decades, there has been increasing integration of the world economy through the increase of international trade. The percentage of world exports has increased significantly relative to world output (Fig. 1.1). However, percentage of world exports declines in 2009, due to global financial crises. Nevertheless, after the eruption of this crisis, the world economy was struggling to recover.

Overview of Central Asian Economies

Following the collapse of the Soviet Union in 1991, the five Central Asian states Kazakhstan, Kyrgyzstan, Tajikistan, Turkmenistan and Uzbekistan became independent countries. After independence, these countries experienced very low or negative economic growth, rising level of poverty, mounting inflation and an increasing unemployment, which was specifically due to breakup in production and market connectivity. In addition, these economies lacked private sector, capital market and had poor infrastructure necessary for market economy. Therefore, it took these economies much time to recover from post independence economic downslide and recovery started to gain momentum (Table 1.3)

Table 1.3: GDP Growth Rate of Central Asian States

Country	2000-06	2007	2008	2009	2010	2011	2012	2013
Kazakhstan	10.3	8.9	3.3	1.2	7.3	7.5	5.0	6.0
Kyrgyzstan	4.0	8.5	8.4	2.9	-0.5	6.0	-0.1	5.5
Tajikistan	9.2	7.6	7.9	3.6	6.5	7.4	7.5	7.4
Turkmenistan	6.0	11.1	14.7	6.1	9.2	14.7	11.1	10.2
Uzbekistan	5.2	9.5	9.0	8.1	8.5	8.3	8.2	8.0

Source: World Bank

By and large Central Asian States recovered economic growth due to regions energy sector, high price of commodities particularly of oil and gas, foreign direct investment, macroeconomic stability and infrastructural development. There have also been structural changes in CAR's due to growth of oil and gas sectors. The success in these stimulated sectors both manufacturing and service sectors effecting the necessary shift and diversification from agricultural sector (Table 1.4).

Table 1.4: Sectoral share in GDP of Central Asian States (Percentage of GDP)

	Agriculture				Industrial				Service			
	2000	2005	2010	2011	2000	2005	2010	2011	2000	2005	2010	2011
Oil Exporting												
Kazakhstan	8.6	6.6	4.7	5.4	40.1	39.2	41.9	40.3	51.3	54.2	53.4	54.3
Turkmenistan	22.9	18.8	12.3	14.5	41.8	37.6	53.5	48.4	35.2	43.6	34.2	37.0
Non-Oil Exporting												
Kyrgyzstan	36.6	31.3	18.7	19.7	31.3	22.0	28.2	27.9	32.1	46.7	53.1	52.4
Tajikistan	27.3	23.8	21.8	27.0	38.4	30.7	27.9	22.4	34.3	45.6	50.3	50.6
Uzbekistan	34.4	28.1	19.8	19.1	23.1	28.8	33.4	32.6	42.5	43.1	46.8	48.3

Source: Asian Development Bank, 2012

The foreign trade has a vital role to play in the economic development in Central Asian States. The external sector contributed fairly to GDP in these newly independent economies (Table 1.5).

Table 1.5: Merchandise Trade as Share of GDP

Years Countries	Exports of Merchandise						Imports of Merchandise					
	percentage of GDP						percentage of GDP					
	1995	2000	2005	2009	2010	2011	1995	2000	2005	2009	2010	2011
Kazakhstan	39.0	56.6	53.5	42.0	44.0	49.0	43.5	49.1	44.7	33.8	29.2	28.0
Kyrgyzstan	29.5	41.8	38.3	54.7	51.6	57.2	42.4	47.6	56.8	78.7	81.7	85.5
Tajikistan	112.0	92.4	54.3	24.5	26.8	---	121.2	100.2	72.8	61.5	59.0	---
Turkmenistan	142.5	95.5	65.0	75.6	74.5	---	145.0	80.9	47.8	45.8	43.4	---
Uzbekistan	31.6	26.5	39.7	35.0	33.1	33.1	28.7	26.7	30.0	29.2	24.5	24.5

Source: *Asian Development Bank, 2012*

The performance of external sector has improved as compared to past. This favourable trade performance since 1995 has been stimulated due to development in metals and minerals sectors in oil exporting countries and by increasing prices of cotton and gold in non-oil exporting countries. Between 1995 and 2010, overall growth of external sector in oil exporting economies was high. However, in non-oil exporting economies, export performance assumed momentum after 2001. In Kyrgyzstan export growth fluctuated from low to strong growth due to fluctuations in gold prices and gold products. Similarly, Uzbekistan and Tajikistan economies continue to recover growth from the exports of aluminium and cotton.

In CAR's the main export and import commodities are shown in table 1.6. The profile of commodities reveals some commonalities across the region. Primarily products (hydrocarbon, metals, cotton and other agricultural products) dominate the structure of exports of all five countries. The export performance appeared to be closely correlated with dynamics on international prices for key commodities. Three countries, which demonstrated very fast growth of exports in the decade (Kazakhstan, Turkmenistan and Uzbekistan), are those rich in hydrocarbon, which enjoyed a major spike in their terms of trade, Kyrgyzstan did not experience any significant change in terms of trade and Turkmenistan's terms of trade deteriorated, and its exports decline.

Table 1.6: Top Export and Import Items of Central Asian States

Kazakhstan	Exports	(a)Crude oil (b) other energy products (c) iron & steel (d) non-ferrous metals (e) ores, radioactive elements (d) precious metals (e) cereals & flour
	Imports	(a)Machines & equipments (b) energy products (c) prepared foods (d) iron & steel & articles thereof (e) chemical products and (f) plastic & rubber.
Kyrgyzstan	Exports	(a)Gold (b) electricity (c) machines & equipments (d) tobacco (e) cotton (f) vegetables & fruits (g) radioactive elements (h) clothing (i) oil products
	Imports	(a)Machines & equipments (b) energy products (c) chemical products (d) products of light industries (e) prepared foods (f) plastic & rubber (g) iron & steel & articles thereof
Tajikistan	Exports	Aluminium (b) energy products (c) electricity (d) vegetable & fruits
	Imports	(a)Alumina (b) electricity (c) machines & equipments (d) oil products (e) vegetable products (f) prepared food (g) metals (h) timber
Turkmenistan	Exports	(a)Natural gas (b) oil products (c) crude oil (d) cotton fibre
	Imports	(a)Machines & equipments (b) prepared food (c) chemical products (d) metals and (e) plastic & rubber
Uzbekistan	Exports	(a)Cotton fibre (b) energy products (c) metals (d) machinery & equipments (e) chemical products (f) food products
	Imports	(a)Energy products (b) metals (c) machinery & equipments (d) chemical products & plastic and (d) food products

Source: *UN COMTRADE*

The total trade balance of oil exporting in CARs was favourable from the last few years due to surplus of trade in Kazakhstan and Turkmenistan, whereas these countries experienced a large deficit in capital account, which was probably due to large investments in oil and natural gas projects. On other side, non-oil exporting countries face unfavourable trade balance.

The CAR's being primarily agrarian economies have large wealth of minerals and metals possess vast potential for trade. Having immense wealth of hydrocarbon resources like oil and gas, these Central Asian countries are also rich in precious and strategic minerals like uranium and gold. Hence, the region has large potential in trade by increasing its exports to earn large earnings.

Overview of Indian Economy

The Indian economy has experienced a structural change from the last two decades. The pace of transformation was limited before reform period, but after introduction of new economic reforms in 1991, it became rapid. After independence, Indian economy was predominantly agricultural. The contribution of primary sector (agricultural, logging, fishing and forestry) in GDP was largest, followed by service and industrial sector respectively. Thereafter, the contributions of industrial and service sector were increased and contribution of agricultural share declined in the national output. Precisely, the contribution of primary sector in GDP decreased from 54.56 percent in 1950 to 28.5 percent in 1994, while contribution of secondary sector was 16.11 percent in 1950, increased to 26.8 percent in 1994. Similarly, the contribution of tertiary sector increased to 44 percent in 1994 from 29percent in 1950 (Economic Survey of India 1995).

Table 1.7: Sectoral Share in GDP of India

Sector	1994	2000	2005	2009	2010	2011
Primary	28.5	23.4	18.8	17.7	17.7	17.2
Secondary	26.8	26.2	28.1	27.6	27.1	26.4
Tertiary	44.7	50.5	53.1	54.7	55.1	56.4

Source: Asian Development Bank (ADB)

The share of primary sector has continuously been decreasing from 23 percent in 2000 to 18.8 percent in 2005 to 17.9 percent in 2009. In 2011, it further decreased to 17.7 percent. The decreasing share of primary sector in national output partially indicates that Indian economy has been experiencing a healthy structural transformation. The secondary sector however did not grow at a speed commensurate with seeming structural transformation as indicated by the dwindling share of primary sector. The contribution of secondary sector shows a marginal change from 26.8 percent in 1994 to 26.2 percent in 2000, to 28.1 percent in 2005, to 26.4 percent in 2011. The expected role of industry in replacing primary sector in terms of output and employment is glaringly missing in the Indian experience. Thus, Indian economy experienced a structural change within industrial sectors, the share of consumer goods decreased and capital goods and basic goods industries decreased in total industrial value added from 1991.

Concerning the contributions of tertiary sector in GDP, it has significantly increased from 44.7 percent in 1994 to 50.5 percent in 2000. In 2005, it was round about 53.1 percent while in 2009 it was at 54.7 percent, which further increased to 56.4 percent in 2011. Indeed tertiary sector constitutes more than half of Indian GDP, making it the first economy in the world to experience such rapid shift from primary sector to tertiary sector.

Against this backdrop, the structure of demand (Table 1.8) has undergone important changes. The private consumption decreased from 64.2 percent in 1995 to 56.0 percent in 2011 and government consumption was marginally increased form 10.8 percent in 1995 to 11.7 percent in 2011. However, the growth acceleration was accompanied with the growth of GDCF, which increased from 25.5 percent in 1995 to 34.3 percent in 2005 to 35.5 percent in 2011. Similarly, rise in exports and imports of goods and services is shown by the figures in the table1.8.

Table 1.8: Structure of Demand Percentage of GDP at Current Market Prices

Structure of Demand	1995	2000	2005	2010	2011
Pvt. Consumption	64.2	63.7	58.3	56.5	56.0
Govt. Consumption	10.8	12.6	10.9	11.9	11.7
Gross Domestic Capital Formation	25.5	24.3	34.3	35.8	35.5
Exports of goods and services	10.0	13.2	19.3	22.8	24.6
Imports of goods and services	10.3	14.2	22.0	26.9	29.8

Source: Asian Development Bank. 2012

After 1990s, with a shift in macro-economic policies which accelerated structural transformation, Indian economy also underwent fundamental change with regard to its external sector. The economy became progressively open to rest of the world. The exports and imports of goods and services doubled from 22.9 percent of GDP in 1991-2000 to 49.8 percent in 2009-2011. Correspondingly, capital flow enhanced from 41.9 percent of GDP in 1991-2000 to 106.5 percent in 2009-2011.

Table 1.9: Openness Indicators (Percentage of GDP)

Items	1991-01	2001-10	2004-08	2009-11
Export plus imports of goods and services	22.9	39.2	40.8	49.8
Current Receipts and payments plus capital Receipts and payments	41.9	78.7	83.5	106.5

Source: Asian Development Bank 2012

The high growth period 2004-08 was accompanied with an increasing merchandise exports, imports, and capital inflows. In addition, percentage net capital inflows increased from 2.2 percent in 1991-2000 to 4.6 percent in

2004-08. The openness of Indian economy improved external position, the debt/GDP ratio decreased from 29 percent to 18.6 percent in 1991-2000 to 2009-2010 respectively. Similarly, debt service also decreased from 24.9 percent in 1991-2000 to 4.7 percent in 2009-2011.

Table 1.10: India's External Sector (Percentage)

Items	1991-00	2001-10	2004-08	2009-11
Balance of Payment				
Exports	8.6	17.7	25.4	15.8
Imports	9.6	19.5	32.3	14.6
Trade/ GDP	-2.8	-5.3	-5.4	-8.6
Current Account Balance/GDP	-1.3	-.0.5	-0.3	-2.6
Net Capital Flows	2.2	3.4	4.6	2.7
External Debt Indicators				
Debt/GDP	29	19	17.7	18.6
Debt /service	24.9	8.8	8.3	4.7

Source: *Indian Economic Survey 2011-12.*

Price stability also contributed to high growth rate of Indian economy. The wholesale price index inflation decreased from 8.1 percent in 1991-2000 to 5.5 percent in the recent period. Again, in 2005-06 all commodities inflation decreased to 4.47 percent, but due to economic crises in 2008, annual average inflation increased from 8.05 percent, to 9.11 percent in 2011-12 (Table 1.11).

Table 1.11: Annual Average Inflation (WPI Percent)

Commodities	2005-06	2006-07	2007-08	2008-09	2009-10	2010-11	2011-12
All Commodities	4.47	6.59	4.74	8.05	3.80	9.55	9.11
Primary commodities	4.30	9.62	8.33	11.05	12.66	18.41	9.91
Fuel and power	13.58	6.46	0.03	11.57	-2.11	12.24	13.67
Manufacturing products	2.42	5.66	4.78	6.16	2.22	5.46	7.58

Source: *Indian Economic Survey 2011-12.*

It is clear from the data here that the primary and fuel products annual inflation remained consistently high from 2008-09. The inflation rate of manufactured products stands stable, but decreased to 2.2 percent in 2009-10, due to global economic crises.

Figure 1.2 presents the weighted share of products to wholesale price index inflation; the primary product has decreased from 46 percent in 2010-11 to 28 percent in 2011-12. However, the contribution of manufactured products increased to 49 percent in 2011-12 from 35 percent in 2010-11. Subsequently, the fuel contribution remains nearly same 19 percent in 2010-11 and 23 percent in 2011-12.

Fig. 1.2: Weighted Share of Products (WPI)

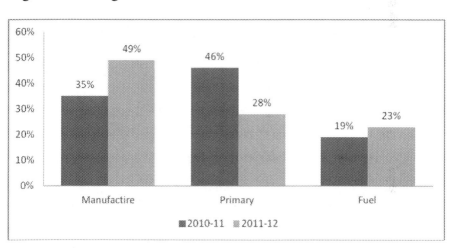

Source: World Trade Organization (WTO) 2012

The overview of the economies of both regions reveals large economic complementarities thereby offers a great scope for trade between the two regions. Based on resource endowments the two regions have large benefits in trading with each other. While CAR's are rich in energy resources, strategic minerals and precious metals, Indian economy offers a long choice of consumer items, like pharmaceuticals etc and quality technology of various kinds relevant to Central Asian economies. In addition, India has a good experience of economic and political transformation. Besides economic resources, this Central Asian region as the immediate neighbourhood is otherwise also vital for India. Hence, good and strong relations between these two regions could be possible and cultivated through good economic and trade relations. In this backdrop, the present study has been undertaken to study India's relation with Central Asian States with special reference to trade.

India has large scope for enhancement of the trade, commerce and investment with Central Asian States; keeping in view, their economic resource endowment and growing consumer market and Central Asian States have great advantage in refurbishing their economies through collaborating with India.

This study mainly concentrates on the economic relationship between India and Central Asian states. Therefore, the study has been carried out keeping in view the following objectives:

1. To study the economic performance of India and Central Asian States since 1991
2. To examine the trade potential of India and Central Asian States
3. To examine the India's trade relations with Central Asian States
4. To analyze the composition and trend in trade between the two regions and
5. To explore the economic sectors with mutual advantage for future cooperation.

Methodology and Data Base

The data used for the study is secondary in nature usually collected from the highly placed sources like World Bank, International Monetary Fund (IMF), Asian Development Bank (ADB), US Energy International Agency (EIA), UCNTAD, COMRADE, Ministry of Commerce, and Govt. of India. Being actively engaged with the economic survey of these countries, the reports on socio-economic variables released by various international agencies and institutions the have been used for analysis. Important variables like per capita income, inflation rate, trade-GDP ratio and their respective compositions were used in conjunction with conventional economic understanding regarding trends in growth and composition of these variables. This helped to explain the impact of external sector on the India and CAR's economies. Besides, it revealed trade and investment potential in these economies.

The data collected from these sources was tabulated, analysed and critically scanned with the help of statistical tools to draw the conclusion in consonance with the objectives of the present study.

Statistical Tools

In the course of this study various econometric techniques has been employed to determine the trade relations between India and CAR's like gravity model of trade, revealed comparative cost advantage, and other descriptive statistics.

Gravity Model

For empirical analysis of trade relations between India and Central Asian States, gravity model have been used to explain balance of trade. The balance of trade is determined by three approaches- the elasticity approach, absorption approach and monetary approach. A model for balance of trade was derives in which all three approaches were employed by Krugman and Baldwin (1987), Rose and Yellen (1989), Baharumshah (2001). The gravity model includes supply of exports and demand for imports. Where demand for imports is depend on income and price. This model is based on the concept of Newton's Law of Universal Gravitation and several economists such as Tinbergen, Poyhonen and Linneman used this concept in international trade. The basic expression is derived as.

$$F = G \frac{m_1 m_2}{r^2}$$

$$Trade_{ij} = \alpha \frac{GDP_i GDP_j}{Distance_{ij}} ---(I)$$

The equation (I) is transformed into a linear form that derives it into usual regression analysis:

$$log\left(Trade_{ij}\right)=\alpha+\beta_1 log\left(GDP_iGDP_j\right)+\beta_2 log\left(Distance_{ij}\right)+u_{ij} ----(II)$$

However, Linneman's use this model on the basis on Walresian General Equilibrium System. The basic models of international trade like Ricardian and the Heckscher & Ohlin are not applicable in multilateral trade (Bergstrand and Egger 2010). The heterogeneity among different trading partners was snub by using panel data analysis or pooled ordinary least square method (OLS). In this connection, Matyas (1997 and 1998) include different dummy variables between trading partners. Van Hove and Abraham (2005) also incorporated these dummy variables in gravity model for Asian countries. The gravity model was analyzed by Krugman (1985) under the assumption of increasing returns to scale in production. The most important theoretical work for gravity model was done by Anderson (1979) based on assumption Cobb Douglas production function and in an appendix, Constant Elasticity of Substitution Preference in connection with differentiation of goods origin (Armington Association). Andersons gravity equation in the form of

$$X_{ij}=\left[\frac{GDP_iGDP_j}{\sum_{j-1}^{N}GDP_J}\right]*\frac{1}{f\left(distance_{ij}\right)}*\left[\left(\sum_{j-1}^{n}\frac{GDP_J}{GDP_w}\right)\left(\frac{1}{f(distance\,tan_{ceij}})\right)\right]$$

Where $f(distance\,tan_{ceij}$ is trade cost

GDP_w is world GDP

X_{ij} is merchandise flow of trade between country i and j

GDP_iGDP_j is current gross domestic product in country i and j.

Bergstrand (1989) extended Helpman and Krugman model with demand and offer functions to explain flow of trade in addition with income per capita for representing capital intensity of trading partners. Bergstrand version of gravity model was complete, including various variables like GDP, Per capita income and distance. However, Anderson and Van Win Coop (2001) augmented this model and included income, distance in addition with per capita income in the gravity equation.

$$\log\left(Trade_{ij}\right)\alpha + \beta_1 \log\left(GNI_i GNI_j\right) + \beta_2 \log\left(PCGNI_i PCGNI_j\right) + \beta_3 \log\left(Dis \tan ce_{ij}\right) + uij --- III$$

Sample Size and Data

To estimate trade potential between India and Central Asian Republics, by using basic gravity model equations to determine the coefficients of trade flow. In addition, we estimate an augmented gravity model by including other variables to examine their impact on trade flows. Finally, the estimated coefficients are analyzed to evaluate trade potential of India with Central Asian Republics. In this study, we have included only five republics of Central Asia Republics such as Kazakhstan, Kyrgyzstan, Tajikistan, Turkmenistan and Uzbekistan. Annual data from 2000 to 2012 was considered, including India's exports to and from CAR's. This data was obtained from Ministry of Commerce, Govt. of India. Data on GDP, GDP per capita were obtained from World Development Indicators (2012) database. Data on distance between capital India and capital of other countries were obtained from www.indo.com.distance.

Revealed Comparative Cost Advantage

We have analyzed bilateral trade of India and CARs with utilizing trade statistics known as Revealed Comparative Advantage (RCA) also known as Balassa Index. This index is used to identify a country's export advantage and disadvantage with respect to the rest of the world in a particular class of goods and services.

RCA of ith country under j^{th} commodity class RCA_{ij} is given below

$$RCA_{ij} = \dfrac{\dfrac{x_{ij}}{x_{it}}}{\dfrac{x_{wj}}{x_{wt}}}$$

The RCA has been computed for India and Central Asia by using the 2 and 4 digit HS commodity classification of year 2012. However, the ratio of RCA is greater or less than one. India has RCA >1 in several items, which India could export to Central Asian States and vice versa.

Descriptive statistics like mean, percentages and proportions has been used to analyse the trade results very correctly.

Structure of the Study

In order to accomplish the above cited objectives, this study has been divided into eight chapters as follows:

Chapter-1, begins with importance of international trade in world's top trading economies like USA, China and High Performance Asian Economies. Moreover, it presents a synoptic picture of the economic profile of Indian and Central Asian State's economies consisting of the pattern of growth, structural transformation, and contribution of external sector in national output, which will serve as a background study to evaluate and derive meaningful relation between India and this region. Chapter - 2, attempts to review the existing literature on both theoretical grounds and empirical evidence, regarding the relation between India and Central Asian States. This chapter therefore, highlights some of the major research gaps that present study seeks to address. Chapter - 3, inculcates discussions on trade and foreign investment policies of India and post Soviet CARs. Indeed, some glimpses of such policies during the Soviet period were offered. Trade relations between India and CARs after the collapse of Soviet Union are discussed in chapter - 4 of the study. Based on the gravity model and revealed comparative advantage index, analysis offered in this chapter presents an estimated trade potential between India and CARs and identifies some of the major commodities that have a comparative trade advantage for both sides. To enhance the trade potential and comparative trade advantage, governments of CARs and India have at times come up with certain joint ventures and economic agreements, which were discussed in the chapter - 5 of study. There is still a huge potential for trade relations between India and CARs such as energy cooperation, which could be a major potential sector for India, given the increasing demands of hydrocarbon. Altogether, the potential such cooperation is discussed in chapter-6 of the study. Nonetheless, such relations are not smooth sailing and involves certain twists and terms, which are debated in the chapter - 7 of the present study. However, to overcome the obstacles of economic relations between India and CARs, some of the interventions are suggested in the chapter - 8.

CHAPTER 2

Literature Overview

The present chapter attempts to review the existing literature in theoretical, historical and empirical perspectives about the India-Central Asia relations. International trade between India and Central Asia has great significance for both sides. The existence of international trade lies in its potential to benefit the participants. Given the institutional and logistic infrastructure, trade generally is a source of prosperity for the economies of the participating states. Nonetheless, the existence and expected expansion of bilateral trade depends on the one hand upon the institutional and infrastructural facilities and at the same time upon the spread and extent of comparative advantages enjoyed by the participants continues in relation to each other. In this connection, some of the important studies vis-à-vis India-Central Asia economic relations are critically discussed under here.

Kazakhstan: Foreign Trade Policy (1998)[1] by Markhamat discusses that Kazakhstan adopted new trade policy after independence, which stimulates its exports and less cost raw materials were available for foreign buyers. Author also highlights that Kazakhstan's market is not capable to compete with foreign

---

[1] M. Khasanova. (1998). 'Kazakhstan: Foreign Trade Policy'. *In:* Boris Rumer and Stanislav Zhukov (eds.), *Central Asia: The Challenges of Independence*. New York: M. E. Sharpe, pp 169-207.

firms. However, author does not point out the economic relation of Kazakhstan with neighbouring after the adoption of new trade policy.

The Emerging Trade Relation between India and Central Asia (1999)[2] by Azhar Mohammad, highlights that economic relation between India and Central Asian republics is presently very low. There has been insignificant trade, limited number of joint ventures and no worthwhile investment in Central Asian region by Indian businessman and industry, though there are small government credit lines. Nevertheless, the potential for mutual economic advantages for the two regions from an enhanced trade and economic relationship is vast. Central Asia is a huge consumer market; both Central Asia and India have economic complementarities in terms of resources, manpower and market. For India, economic cooperation is possible through joint ventures in banking, insurance, and agriculture, and information technology.

Reassessing a New Great Game between India and China in Central Asia by Jen-Kun (2000)[3], discusses that in the New Great Game of Central Asia, three players are most active such as Russia, China and the United States. Other small players include Iran and India. Author points out that US interest in Central Asia increased only after 9/11 attack. Even though U.S was interested towards this region before the attack, but this incidence involved U.S quickly. As we know energy demands are getting heavier globally for sustaining industrial output, great powers of the world including the U.S, China, Russia and India are increasingly focusing towards this region keenly. However, it is not pointed out in the study that India is not active participants in Central Asia due to facing many challenges in Central Asia such as land route connectivity and instability in neighbouring countries, while as China and Russia are not facing these problems.

India and Central Asia: Cultural, Economic and Political Links by Gopal (2001)[4] emphasised that India's relationship with newly independent CARs

---

2   A. Muhammad. (1999). 'The Emerging Trade Relation between India and Central Asia'. *In:* Shami-u-din (eds.), *Nationalism in Russia and central Asian Republics*. New Delhi: Lancers Book, pp. 329-341.

3   Jen-Kun Fu (2000). Reassessing a New Great Game between India and China in Central Asia, *China and Eurasian Forum Quarterly*. 8 (1): 17-22

4   G. Surender. (2001). 'India and Central Asia: Cultural, Economic and Political Links'. New Delhi: Shipra Publications, pp. 5-20.

are admirable, have historic and cultural relations, mainly from breakdown of Soviet Union. During 16th and 17th centuries, Indian traders in Uzbekistan were able to gain access to trade centres in Central Asia. The study identifies that economic relation between India and CARs are continuously with numerous obstacles.

India and Central Asia by Bedi (2002)[5] emphasized that in the current scenario India is in quest of to widen relationship with CARs based on number of common grounds including secularism and democracy. Indeed, both sides have cordial and friendly relations and India's present diplomatic presence in this region would explore future energy requirement for India.

Joshi (2003)[6] discussed that in all industrial countries energy demand is growing. Similarly, India is also face this problem, though it increasingly looking to Central Asia both as a reliable source energy resources and having strategic interest in Central Asia. Apart from oil and natural gas newly independent states are important for national security of India, particularly for combating terrorism. Author highlights in the study the potential areas for cooperation included IT, telecom, biotechnology, service sector and education. Similarly, tourism has potential for cooperation, which increases people-to-people contacts. However, India is facing faltering competition in this region. Therefore, this competition would adversely affect India's policy and diplomacy in this region, if competition remains dominant, India would have to take hard decisions.

Studying *India Joins the Great Game: Indian Strategy in Central Asia*, by Blank (2004)[7] has illustrates that India develops its association with CARs through economic, political and military relations. In the study author argues that India's growing relations has not significance only in combating terrorism,

---

5   Rahul Bedi. (2002). India and Central Asia. *Frontline*. 19(19). Available on http://www.Flonnet.com/fl1919/19190600.htm. (accessed on 20 March 2011).

6   N. Joshi. (2003). Introduction. *In:* Nirmala Joshi (eds.), *Central Asia: The Great Game Replayed, An Indian Perspective.* New Delhi: New Centure Publications, pp. 1-10.

7   Stephen Blank (2004). 'India Joins the Great Game: Indian Strategy in Central Asia'. *In:* Indranil Banerjie (eds.), *India and Central Asia.* UK: Brunel Academic Publishers, 261-301.

drug trafficking, but it has profound strategic and economic roots. He also highlights energy resources in CARs have great implication for India.

India-Central Asia Energy Cooperation (2004)[8] by Sudha discusses that Central Asia has chunk of energy resources and it is considered as a potential transit corridor for Asian markets as a result it became a playground for regional players, but India is spectator despite having growing demand for energy. No doubt, the geographic location of Central Asia may be constraints for India, but it has a huge demand for developing energy infrastructure.

Jatar (2004)[9], in his study *Indian Energy Strategies and Central Asia* argues that it is important for India to keep in view the ground realities of economies of the region. These economies are by and large, poor and fall in the category of low developing countries and face dual challenges of substantially adjustment and economic rebuilding. External assistance will help these economies to achieve their potential at a faster pace and it is here that India has the opportunity for making investment in certain sectors. Author expressed in the study that high-level visits between India and Central Asia nations were exchanged on a regular basis additionally with trade exhibitions and visits of trade delegations. In this respect, Indian investors are encouraged to enter into this region. In the present study author discusses that large oil explorations, drilling and pipeline projects have been signed, if these agreement would be implemented, India could bid for bigger energy projects. However, author ignores the negative impact of external assistance, wherein foreign firms invest only for profit motive.

Jacob's *India's Overseas Energy Policy: The Central Asian Factor, in Central Asia: Present Challenges and Future Prospects* (2005)[10] discusses that India's energy demand is increasing more than its domestic supply with 70 percent

8   Mahalingam. (2004). 'India-Central Asia Energy Cooperation'. *In:* K. Santhanam and Ramakant Dwivedi (eds.), *India and Central Asia: Advancing the Common Interest*. New Delhi: Anamaya Publishers, pp.111-143.

9   N. Jatar. (2004). 'Indian Energy Strategies and Central Asia'. *In:* Indranil Banerjie (eds.), *India and Central Asia*. UK: Brunel Academic Publishers Ltd, pp. 302-325.

10   J. Happymon. (2005). 'India's Overseas Energy Policy: The Central Asian Factor'. *In:* V. Nagendra Rao and Mohammad Monir Alam (eds.), *Central Asia: Present Challenges and Future Prospects*. New Delhi: Knowledge World, pp. 315-322.

of oil being imported from international market particularly from the Gulf countries. But due to fragile situation in these countries, India faces oil crises, which manifest that Central Asian region, could prove to be the viable alternative for India to reduce its energy dependence from volatile countries.

Central Asia's Security: the Asian Dimension by Patnaik (2005)[11] holds that Central Asian region has great importance in the world due to its geostrategic location and has rich energy resources. However, instability in Afghanistan is mainly regarded as a cause of probable threats to other countries of the world because illegal drug trafficking and production also includes terrorism. In this present study author suggests that regional cooperation in Central Asia and Eurasia could become an important factor for the maintenance of peace and security in the region, in turn it would stable economic growth and development. Indeed, India has relevance in CARs because having experience in economic and political transformation.

The Caspian Great Game: Geopolitics of Oil and Natural Gas by Asopa (2006)[12] highlights that Caspian Sea has ownership problem that retards the full utilization of energy reserves of this sea. On the other hand, the author focuses only on oil and gas reserves in Caspian Sea. The possible pipeline routes are discussed in this study, but it is not discussed that pipeline routes are depend upon stability in neighbouring countries.

Central Asia and South Asia: Potential of India's Multilateral Economic Diplomacy in Inter-Regional Cooperation by Mavlonov (2006)[13] focused on regional cooperation and emphasized that India has capability to promote economic cooperation between South-Central Asia. In this study, author explains the present bilateral trade of India with South-Central Asian countries and discussed that only India is suitable for regional cooperation, but this is not fact.

---

[11]   A. Patnaik. (2005). 'Central Asia's Security: the Asian Dimension'. *In:* R. R. Sharma (eds.), *India and Emerging Asia*. New Delhi: Sage Publication, pp. 206-231

[12]   K. Asopa. (2006). 'The Caspian Great Game: Geopolitics of Oil and Natural Gas'. *In:* K. Sheel (eds.), *Struggle for Spheres of Interest in Trans-Caucasia-Central Asia and India's Stakes: An Appraisal of India's Central Asia Policy*. New Delhi: Manak Publication Pvt. Ltd, pp 175-229.

[13]   M. Ibrokhim (2006). Central Asia and South Asia: Potential of India's Multilateral Economic Diplomacy in Inter-Regional Cooperation, *Strategic Analysis*. 30(2): 424-448

The consensuses of all countries are necessary for regional cooperation. However, the regional powers have conflict with each other, India is looking Central and South Asia through the prism of U.S while as Pakistan through China. These are important responsible factors for deteriorating regional cooperation.

India's Economic Diplomacy Trends with Central Asia: The Potential and Priorities (2007)[14] by Maylonov discussed that India has age-old relationship with Central Asian Region and were great powerful centres during ancient times and Silk Route facilitates economic relation that times. In the current scenario, India's relations with Central Asia are minimal but India is seeking to revive this relations. Both sides are trying to enhance relationship as result embassies were established and exchanges of high-level visits were given a space. Indeed today, the economic relation of India with this region has great significance because of rich energy resources and growing favourable investment climate. Central Asia could also reap benefits due to these relations.

The Growth of Diplomatic Relations Between Kazakhstan and India (2007)[15] by Utegenova discusses that India was first country to establish diplomatic relations with Kazakhstan after independence. As a result, among Central Asian States Kazakhstan is major trading partner of India. The growing bilateral trade between India and Kazakhstan will benefit both nations on the basis of potential areas such as IT, pharmaceuticals and defence in India and hydrocarbon in Kazakhstan. Whereas author has not used any economic index to identify potential areas and commodities.

India-Kazakhstan Economic Relations (2007)[16] by Gidadhubli said that Kazakhstan is major trading partner of India in Central Asian republics and

---

[14]   M. Ibrokhim. (2007). 'India's Economic Diplomacy Trends with Central Asia: The Potential and priorities'. *In:* Anuradha M. Chenoy and Ajay Patnaik (eds.), *Commonwealth of Independent States: Energy, Security and Development*. New Delhi: Knowledge World, pp. 279-296.

[15]   A. Utegenova. (2007). 'The Growth of Diplomatic Relations Between Kazakhstan and India'. *In:* Santhanam, Kuralay Baizakova and Ramakant Dwivedi (eds.), *India-Kazakhstan Perspectives: Regional and International Interaction*. New Delhi: Anamaya publishers, pp. 20-29.

[16]   R. Gidadhubli. (2007). 'India-Kazakhstan Economic Relations'. *In:* K. Santhanam, Kuralay Baizakova and Ramakant Dwivedi (eds.), *India-Kazakhstan Perspectives: Regional and International Interaction*, New Delhi: Anamaya publishers, pp. 30-39.

this country can play important role in meeting growing energy demand of India. However, the author also includes both challenges and opportunities in this paper. This author emphasized more on Kazakhstan while as Uzbekistan and Turkmenistan has same importance as Kazakhstan.

India and Kazakhstan: Building Energy Bridges by Mahalingam (2007)[17], overviews energy scenario of Kazakhstan and India, and highlights potential areas of energy cooperation. However, the author does not focus that China and Russia has strong foothold in Kazakhstan as compared to India.

Regional Economic Cooperation and Integration in Central Asia by Sachdeva (2007)[18] concentrates regional economic cooperation in Central Asian States would reduce their dependence on foreign countries. They could exchange goods and services within the region that can benefit all participating countries. However, it is not explained in this paper that comparatively all new independent states have comparative advantage in energy products. In this respect, this region has to maintain cordial relations also with their neighbouring countries for exporting surplus energy products and import consumer and capital goods.

Geopolitics Perspectives on Central Asia: An Indian View by Nirmala Joshi (2007)[19], portrays that geopolitics of Central Asia is immediate concern to India. Nevertheless, author postulates Pakistan as a major challenge for India, but ignores other challenges such as China, Russia and land route connectivity.

Politics of Oil and natural Gas in Central Asia- Conflict and Co-operation by Gidadhubli (2007)[20] discusses that energy plays vital role for the economic

---

[17] M. Sudha. (2007). 'India and Kazakhstan: Building Energy Bridges'. *In:* K. Santhanam, Kuralay Baizakova and Ramakant Dwivedi (eds.), *India-Kazakhstan Perspectives: Regional and International Interaction.* New Delhi: Anamaya publishers, pp. 47-63.

[18] G. Sachdeva. (2007). 'Regional Economic Cooperation and Integration in Central Asia'. *In:* K. Santhanam, Kuralay Baizakova and Ramakant Dwivedi (eds.), *India-Kazakhstan Perspectives: Regional and International Interaction.* New Delhi: Anamaya publishers, pp. 111-124.

[19] N. Joshi. (2007). 'Geopolitics Perspectives on Central Asia: An Indian View'. *In:* J. N. Roy and B. B. Kumar (eds.), *India and Central Asia: Classical to Contemporary Periods.* New Delhi: Concept Publishing Company, pp 143-155.

[20] R. Gidadhubli. (2007). 'Politics of Oil and natural Gas in Central Asia-Conflict and

development of Central Asian States. These states rely heavily on energy resources for future economic prosperity. For that reason, these countries need to diversify existed pipelines towards the new market. However, the author has focused only on the positive side of energy resources. It is not possible for any economy to sustain its long-term economic growth on one sector of the economy. Number of study highlights that Dutch Disease would affect the entire CARs.

Economic Changes in Central Asia and Indian Response by Sachdeva (2007)[21] discusses that in 1991, new independent states of Central Asia such as Kazakhstan, Kyrgyzstan, Tajikistan, Turkmenistan and Uzbekistan transform their economic system from central to market oriented in varying degrees as a result Kazakhstan and Kyrgyzstan progressed much faster than rest of the countries. The author also pointed out that after disintegration of Soviet Union, Central Asian countries were facing high inflation, output declined, high transport costs and collapse of traditional market. However, the author does not highlight that Russia's monopoly remains even after breakup and today Russia is major trading partner. Author accentuates that these countries succeed due to market-oriented strategy, but the author did not show in what area the Central Asian states succeed. Lastly, author explained Indian response towards Central Asia after adoption of new economic policy in 1991.

Indo-Tajik Relations: A Historical Perspective by Kaw (2007)[22] outlines the historical relations between India-Central Asia and number of important scholars are pointed out who came from Central Asia to India such as Shah Ali Hamadan who spread Islam in Kashmir etc. The author highlights that number of commodities were traded but their value and name were not discussed. Indeed present bottlenecks of trade are not highlighted in this

Co-operation'. *In:* J. N. Roy and B. B. Kumar (eds.), *India and Central Asia: Classical to Contemporary Periods*. New Delhi: Concept Publishing Company, pp. 156-171.

[21]   G. Sachdeva. (2007). 'Economic Changes in Central Asia and Indian Response'. *In:* J. N. Roy and B. B. Kumar (eds.), *India and Central Asia: Classical to Contemporary Periods*. New Delhi: Concept Publishing Company, pp. 251-272

[22]   M. A. Kaw. (2007). 'Indo-Tajik Relations: A Historical Perspective'. *In:* K Santhanam and Ramakant Dwivedi (eds.), *India-Tajikistan Cooperation: Perspectives and Prospects*. New Delhi: Anamaya Publishers, pp. 8-20

study. Nonetheless, author emphasises that past relations would be helpful for building future relations between India-Central Asia particularly with Tajikistan.

India–Central Asia Relations: Quest for Energy Security by Laxmi (2007)[23], explains that India's economic growth requires energy inputs for industrial development. The demand and supply gap of energy in India is increasing; as a result, it is now dependent on energy imports. However, the energy security has becoming comprehensive. This study emphasis on energy resources of Central Asia as an alternative and future source for India. Nevertheless, it is not mentioned in this study that Central Asia is not energy source for only India but also for major powers of the world like European Union and the U. S. Particularly U.S attempts to engage the Central Asian Republics through economic and security cooperation.

India-Central: The Quadrilateral Framework (2008)[24] by Ajay Patnaik highlights that Chinese route is alternative for India to access Central Asia; it also connects power grids of this region with India through Chinese grids. However, India is negotiating for gas pipeline with Iran, Pakistan and Russia supports this gas pipelines project. The regional stability and economic growth depends upon the South Asia-Eurasia-Iran-China cooperation.

Indo-Kyrgyz Relations: The Search for New Horizons by Pandey (2008)[25] explained that India and Central Asia have historical relations through Silk Route. Both sides try to deepen their age-old relations. As a result, number of visits has been exchanged at ministerial level. India gives most favoured nation status and provides credit lines to Kyrgyzstan. Additionally India has economic and technical relations with this nation. However, author has not highlighted that in Central Asian region, the presence of Russia and China is growing and

---

23   Vijay Laxmi. (2007). India–Central Asia Relations: Quest for Energy Security, *Dialogue*. 8(4): 174-183.

24   A. Patnaik. (2008). 'India-Central: The Quadrilateral Framework'. *In:* P. L. Dash (eds.), *Emerging Asia in Focus: Issues and Problems*. New Delhi: Academic Excellence, pp. 1-11.

25   S. Pandy. (2008). 'Indo-Kyrgyz Relations: The Search for New Horizons'. *In:* K Santhanam and Ramakant Dwivedi (eds.), *India-Kyrgyz Relation Perspectives and Prospects*. New Delhi: Anamaya Publishers, pp. 1-15.

both nations capture maximum market due to production of low priced goods and services as compared to India.

India and Kazakhstan: Emerging Ties by Roy (2008)[26], reveals the emerging ties between India and Kazakhstan. Specifically, author describes that there are various factors such as historical relation, the strategic situation and economic potential, that pave the way for the emergence of a unique relationship between India and Central Asian Republics. Among Central Asia States, Kazakhstan is the second largest republic of the former Soviet Union and holds a special place in India's policy priorities. Over the period of last ten years, the relations between the two countries have developed in a unique and specific way. During this period the objectives of India's policy has been to establish dynamic and multifaceted bilateral relations with Kazakhstan. Author suggested that although there are problems in transporting resources, both countries need to work together to establish some kind of bilateral or multilateral arrangements to transport these resources. In this study author, however does not discuss about the instability of Afghanistan, which is major hindrance for trade between India and Central Asia.

Structural Reforms, Macroeconomic policies and the Future of Kazakhstan by Gillies (2009)[27], presents a small macro model of Kazakhstan to study the impact of various economic policies. The stimulation provides insight into the role of tight monetary policy, higher FDI, rising nominal wages and crude oil prices. The aim of this study has been to give an overview of Kazakh economy over the period of transition and consequence of several economic policies made by authorities. Essentially the main findings of this study are policy reforms accompanied with institutional transformations that imply changes in Kazakhstan's economic structure. However, the contribution of external sector is not included in this study.

Somewhat similarly, Talmiz's study *Geopolitics of Central Asia's Oil and Gas Resources Implication for India's Energy Security* (2010)[28] reveals the need of

---

26   M. Roy. (2008). India and Kazakhstan: Emerging Ties, *Strategic Analysis*. 26 (1): 48-64

27   Gilles Dufrenot. (2009) *Structural Reforms, Macroeconomic policies and the Future of Kazakhstan*, ERUDITE, University de Paris 12 and GREQAM, Marseille.

28   T. Ahmad. (2010). 'Geopolitics of Central Asia's Oil and Gas Resources Implication

energy efficiency on the part of India and the subsequent importance of CARs in meeting the energy demand. With regard to this author has also discussed the significance of Gulf countries. The author while discussing the significance of Gulf countries, make mention about the India's crude oil decreases and subsequent rise in its demand for oil. The demand for oil increased from 122 million tones in 2001-02 to 196 million tones in 2011-12 and expected to further increase in the near future. Hence, due to growing consumption, India is highly depending on imported energy resources. Currently Gulf countries provide two-third India's oil requirements. Nevertheless, the uprisings in Gulf region impacts world oil price, that leads to inflation in energy consuming nations. Therefore, for fulfilling the need of energy, India needs to look towards CAR's.

Russia facing China and India in Central Asia: Cooperation, Competition and Hesitation by Laruelle (2010)[29] is another study emphasizing the great game in Eurasian landmass. Although this research work does not deal with the economic relations between India and CARs, but given its subtle contents vis-à-vis India's presence in CARs, this study reveals some key notions regarding the rise of China and India in Central Asia. Author considers China as a key player, for better or for worse, while as India has potential but latecomer. China has strong foothold in Central Asia as compared to India however, its presence in this region is contested by Russia, even if both have same views regarding geopolitics of Central Asia. Since CAR's are uncomfortable with Muslim extremism, drug trafficking and state failure, both Moscow and Beijing support government of these states. On the one hand, Beijing is against Islamism in Central Asia but on the other side, it has close relation with Pakistan. As a result, Moscow has double standard policy towards China. Therefore, Central Asia is important component for both countries. Where as Russia welcome and support New Delhi for deepening its involvement in Central Asia States.

---

for India's Energy Security'. *In:* Mushtaq Ahmad Kaw (eds.), *Central Asia in Retrospect and Prospect.* New Delhi: Readworthy, pp. 133-148.

29 L. Marlene. (2010). 'Russia Facing China and India in Central Asia: Cooperation, Competition and Hesitation'. *In:* Marlene Laruelle, Jean-Francois Huchet, Sebastien Peyrouse and Bayram Balci, *China and India in Central Asia: A New Great Game.* New York: Palgrave Macmillan, pp. 9-24.

Unlike China, Moscow has cordial foreign policy towards India, because both are against Muslim extremism and Pakistan. Russia has no objection about the involvement of India in Central Asia and providing military training to Tajik, Turkmen and Uzbek officers against international terrorism.

The Afghan and Regional Strategy: The Indian Factor (2010)[30] by Roy elaborates that India as a regional power has strategic interest in Afghanistan. Instability in Afghanistan affects India directly. However, Taliban also impede developmental work being carried out by India in Afghanistan. Several times Indian embassy was attacked in Afghanistan, in response of this India do not break down its relation with Afghanistan. India is biggest partner of this nation in the construction sector and in other developmental projects and develops its relation with Afghanistan only for strategic location and to entry Central Asian region. Instability in Afghanistan delays oil and gas pipeline projects while, as its stability could enhance the regional cooperation.

India and Central Asia: Redefining Energy and Trade Links by Sarma (2010)[31] highlights on hydrocarbon resources of CARs combined with energy need of India. Energy sector including other potential areas such as textiles, IT, tourism, pharmaceuticals, building and food processing has wide scope cooperation between India and CARs. On the other hand, author has also discussed in this study about the significance of North-South Transport corridor project and other alternative routes and also suggested that in the current geo-political situation, India's engagement towards this region should more dynamic.

Great Powers Politics: India's Absence from Ideological Energy Diplomacy in Central Asia by Shen (2010)[32] discusses how and why India failed to compete with other great powers in Central Asia. Author mentioned that global powers

[30]   M. Singh Roy. (2010). 'The Afghan and Regional Strategy: The Indian Factor'. *In:* Marlene Laruelle, Jean-Francois Huchet, Sebastien Peyrouse and Bayram Balci (eds.), *China and India in Central Asia: A New Great Game.* New York: Palgrave Macmillan, pp. 60-80.

[31]   A. Sarma. (2010). India and Central Asia: Redefining Energy and Trade Links. New Delhi: Pentagon Press, pp. 1-132.

[32]   S. Simon. (2010). Great Powers Politics: India's Absence from Ideological Energy Diplomacy in Central Asia, *China and Eurasia forum Quarterly.* 8 (1): 95-110.

have energy interest in this region. These players such as Russia, China and United States are strongly competing each other in this region and other players including Japan and India. Russia and China has strong stakeholders as compared to United States. However, India is also trying to make strong relations with this region, established embassies in all newly independent states, having fully owned and joint ventures. Similarly, pipeline projects are under consideration. The situation of Pakistan and Afghanistan is not pointed out in the study, which is one of the major obstacles for India. The Taliban defeats British, Russia and now United States. Thus, instability in Afghanistan and Pakistan affects India directly.

Foreign Policy and Myth-Making (2011)[33] by Laruelle highlights that global players has interest in five post-Soviet States or as "Greater Central Asia" whereby it also includes Afghanistan. Consequently, there has been a fight among great powers to maintain their presence in this region. In this context given India's age old relations specifically by reasserting the past through revival of "Silk Route."

Perception and strategies: India's Relation with Central Asian Region (2011)[34] by Sengupta discusses that Indian policy analysts want to develop cooperation with regional powers like Russia, China and Iran in addition with Central Asian States. This broader regional cooperation is optimal solution for long-term economic development and will be favourable for implementation of pipeline projects. The author also highlights that Central Asian region is partner of India to control extremist activities in the region. On the other hand, India's engagement with this region will be fruitful; they are not competitive but complementary.

Domestic and International Articulation of the Indian Involvement in Central Asia (2011)[35] Peyrouse, articulates that in 1990s, India has transformed its

---

[33]   L. Marlene. (2011). 'Foreign Policy and Myth-making: Great Game, Heartland and Silk Roads'. *In:* Marlene laruelle and Sebastien Peyrouse (eds.), *Mapping Central Asia: Indian Perception and Strategies*, USA: Ashgate, pp. 7-20.

[34]   S. Anita. (2011). 'Perception and strategies: India's Relation with Central Asian Region'. *In:* Marlene Laruelle and Sebastien Peyrouse (eds.), *Mapping Central Asia: Indian Perception and Strategies.* USA: Ashgate, pp.47-60.

[35]   P. Sebastien. (2011). 'Domestic and International Articulation of the Indian

economy and at the same time Soviet Union disappeared, which adversely affected India in such terms as loss of economic support, market shrinks for Indian exports and the collapse of the "Rupee Trade System". As a result, India was not able to maintain historical relations with newly independent states of Central Asia. Even today, India has not fulfilled the objective of "Look North Policy" and the actual trade level with CAR's is below than its potential level. Very few Indian firms and business enterprises are present in the CAR's market particularly energy sectors. India has cordial relations with Russia and United States that would help to develop relation with CAR's. Their relations will integrate India-Russia-Central Asia, India- USA-Central Asia and it is expected for India-China-CAR's relations.

Indo-Central Asian Economic Relations (2011)[36] by Sachdeva focused that in 1991, India adopted outward oriented strategy as a result India is now fastest growing economy in the world. The deepening of international relation of India's with the rest of the world in general and Asian economies in particular contributes India's external sector. India diversify economic relation from outside Asia to Asian market, in turn India links with South and southeast Asian countries with the establishment of SAFTA, BISMSTE, India-ASEAN agreements and also signed bilateral agreements with Sri Lanka, Singapore, Afghanistan, Nepal etc. Similarly, India builds relations with Pakistan, Afghanistan and Central Asia. India's economic strategies for involving Pakistan, Afghanistan and Central Asia for regional cooperation will impacts positively on all Asian countries. However, the relation between India and Central Asia depends upon the stability of Afghanistan and this nation plays a vital role for facilitating regional economic cooperation that will also reinforce India's objective of Look East policy, and also be helpful for under consideration developmental projects like TAPI and IPI.

Involvement'. *In:* Marlene laruelle and Sebastien Peyrouse (eds.), *Mapping Central Asia: Indian Perception and Strategies*. USA: Ashgate, pp. 75-90.

[36] G. Sachdeva. (2011). 'Indo-Central Asian Economic Relations'. *In:* Marlene laruelle and Sebastien Peyrouse (ed.), *Mapping Central Asia: Indian Perception and Strategies*. USA: Ashgate, pp. 122-140.

India's Policy towards Central Asia: The Pakistan Factor (2011)[37] Roy highlights that major powerful countries have strategic interest in Central Asian region. The new independent states of this region provide opportunities as well as challenges for South Asian region. In the South Asian region, competition arise between India and China, both are energy hungry, in this respect Central Asia is opportunity for both countries. China has acquired good position in this region as compared with India. While as India is keenly focusing towards this region but Pakistan is big hurdle. In South Asia, India and Pakistan are two important countries having nuclear weapons, both are focusing and having different foreign policy towards Central Asia. It is difficult for India to enhance relations with Central Asia without cooperation with Pakistan. India has dire need to change economic policy framework in which Central Asia, Afghanistan and Pakistan fulfil energy security of India.

Kazakhstan's Energy Policy and Cooperation with India by Oxana (2011)[38] highlights that energy collaboration is one of the important area wherein India and Kazakhstan cooperation would gain. Apart from oil and gas it has atomic and thermo-nuclear power engineering, reserves of uranium. Additionally, it possesses the technologies of the production of fuel "tablets". Nevertheless, Russia and China could easily access to this region compared to India. In this respect, Indian Prime Minister Dr. Manmohan Singh had warned in 2005 that, "China is ahead of us in planning for its energy security- India can no longer be complacent." In this respect, India has been in the hunt for access to Kazakhstan's oil and gas projects like IPI and TAPI, but India-Pakistan rivalry made these projects complicated. India has also increased its military and political relation with Russia, investing in Sakhalin Island and Russian-Kazakh Kurmangazy oilfields in the Caspian Sea. Author mentions the views of many experts in this study that Russia gives chance to India and China to

---

[37] M. Singh. (2011). 'India's Policy towards Central Asia: The Pakistan Factor'. *In:* Marlene Laruelle and Sebastien Peyrouse (eds.), *Mapping Central Asia: Indian Perception and Strategies.* USA: Ashgate, pp. 161-178.

[38] O. Dolzhikova. (2011). 'Kazakhstan's Energy Policy and Cooperation with India'. *In:* K. Warikoo (eds.), *Central Asia and South Asia Energy Cooperation and Transport Linkages.* New Delhi: Pentagon Press, pp. 77-85

enhance their cooperation with CARs, because Russia is attempting to reduce the space for the US in this region.

Framing Indo-Central Asian Relations, 1990s-2000s (2011)[39] a study by Patnaik discusses that after 1991, India opened embassies in new independent states of Central Asia and also paid high level exchange of visits to this region. India provides credit lines to Central Asian States in order to purchase Indian goods; in addition, these credit lines were extended over time. However, the Afghanistan is main obstacle for enhancing India-Central Asia relations; the rising up of Taliban in Afghanistan changed the geopolitical situation in South-Central Asia. As a result, India develops security relations with Central Asian States. Nonetheless, India enhances economic relation with this region in defence and energy sectors. India also tries to extended neighbourhood with Central Asia and Afghanistan, but facing competition with regional players.

In her study *India-Central Asia Energy Cooperation* (2012)[40] Nirmala Joshi focuses on increasing energy demand of the world and its impact on Central Asia, particularly of India. After 1990's, energy security occupy the centre stage of international politics. In the past only industrial countries, consume high energy but now-a-days the demand for energy consumption has increased in both industrial and developing countries. To fill the energy deficiency gap these countries focus towards Central Asian Republics. The competition increases in this region due to rich energy resources as a result big powers are playing game in this region. The energy security issue became vital factor that shifts international politics from Europe to Asia.

India and the importance of Central Asia by Pandey (2012)[41], discuss that the Central Asia is important for India given the historical-cultural, geopolitical, and economic proximity of the region. During Soviet times, relations between

---

[39] A. Patnaik. (2011). 'Framing Indo-Central Asian Relations1990s-2000s'. *In:* Marlene Laruelle and Sebastien Peyrouse (eds.), *Mapping Central Asia: Indian Perception and Strategies.* USA: Ashgate, pp. 90-108.

[40] N. Joshi. (2012). 'India-Central Asia Energy Cooperation'. *In:* P. L. Dash (eds.), *India and Central Asia: Two Decades of Transition.* New Delhi: Oxford University Press, pp. 50-61

[41] S. Kumar. (2012). 'India and the importance of Central Asia'. *In:* P. L. Dash (eds.), *India and Central Asia: Two Decades of Transition.* New Delhi: Oxford University Press, pp. 1-11.

India and Central Asia were through Centre that is Moscow. However, after the disintegration of Soviet Union, India changed its foreign policies towards Central Asia and sought to develop political and economic relations. As a result, India established diplomatic relations with Kazakhstan, Kyrgyzstan, Tajikistan, Turkmenistan and Uzbekistan. Indeed there is a competition among great powers of the world particularly Russia, China, Turkey, Iran, Pakistan and US to maintain their presence in region. This geopolitical significance of Central Asia creates problems for India to develop relation with the CARs. Another major obstacle for India to maintain relations with CARs is instability in Afghanistan. However, such geopolitical issues as author has mentioned hinder India's economic relations with CARs, but it is noteworthy that good relations between India and Pakistan are paramount for enhancing relations with Central Asian States.

As for as India's energy demand is concerned, it is sixth energy consuming country in the world and imports more 60 percent of oil from Gulf countries. However, due to fragile situation in Middle East and Persian Gulf countries, India diversifies its sources of energy. India is accessing towards CAR's as an alternative energy source and several projects are under consideration such as TAPI, IPI.

Warikoo's study *India and Central Asia: Potential Implication for Power Rivalries in Eurasia*, (2012)[42] highlights that after the disintegration of Soviet Union, countries such as China, Russia, West and South Asian countries stimulates attention and interest towards CAR's. Simultaneously, CAR's also developed multilateral international network through becoming member of United Nations (UN), Common Wealth of Independent States (CIS), Economic Cooperation Organization (ECO), Organisation of Islamic Cooperation (OIC), Organisation for Security and Co-operation in Europe (OSCE) for self-reliance and independence. In such initiatives, South Asia was also given a consideration wherein India retains a significant position. In fact, CARs are very much keen to transport oil and gas to South Asia through Afghanistan,

---

[42]   K. Warikoo (2012). 'India and Central Asia: Potential Implication for Power Rivalries in Eurasia'. *In:* P. L. Dash (eds.), *India and Central Asia: Two Decades of Transition.* New Delhi: Oxford University Press, pp. 98-116.

but presently Afghanistan's geopolitical scenario is a major obstacle for such trade exchanges, particularly in construction of pipelines.

Based on gravity model, Farrukh and Yunus's *Who is Trading Well in Central Asia? A Gravity Analysis of Exports from the Regional Powers to the Region* (2012)[43] reveals that the regional powers of Asia such as China, India, Iran, Russia, and Turkey have endeavoured to export commodities to Central Asia. Authors analyzes the actual trade and potential trade between these countries and shows that China and Turkey have higher potential of export to Central Asia compared to rest of the countries. Moreover, authors have used basic variables of model in addition with other dummy variables. Still it did not explain why some countries have high potential while others not.

Perspective on Silk Road Connect between Central and South Asia by Khalmatova (2013)[44] explained that loss that hammering of the importance of the "Silk Road" decreased the cooperation between Central and South Asia. Moreover, this cooperation further minimised due to the instability in Afghanistan. Nevertheless, revival of New Silk Road could enhance relations among India-Pakistan-Afghanistan-CARs. On the other hand, projects like TAPI, IPI and transport corridor have significant potential of strengthening trade and economic relations between South-Central Asia regions.

How and Why Scholars Assign a Weighty Role for India in Central Asia by Mavlanova (2013)[45] discusses that India's economic and energy projects in addition with transport corridors and modern technology are main instruments for foretelling into the CARs. Even though they have historical relation through Silk Road, which transfer cultures, religious and political

---

[43]   Farrukh and Yunus (2012). Who is Trading Well in Central Asia? A Gravity Analysis of Exports from the Regional Powers to the Region, *Eurasian Journal of Business and Economics.* 5(9): 21-43.

[44]   U. Khalmatova. (2013). 'Perspective on Silk Road Connect between Central and South Asia'. *In:* R. Malhotra, P. L. Dash, and S. Gill. (eds.), *South and Central Asia: Quest for Peace and Cooperation.* Chandigarh: Centre for Research in Rural and Industrial Development, pp. 31-38.

[45]   D. Mavlanova. (2013). 'How and Why Scholars Assign a Weighty Role for India in Central Asia'. *In:* R. Malhotra, P. L. Dash, and S. Gill. (eds.), *South and Central Asia: Quest for Peace and Cooperation.* Chandigarh: Centre for Research in Rural and Industrial Development, pp. 39-46.

forces, while as revival of this road has great significance even today. Author mentioned in the study that India's economic strength could play a vital role for the stability and economic security of the Central Asian region. Because India's macroeconomic stability and experience in the Asian market promote active economic engagement in the CARs. India could prove to be a substantial source of economic security and stability in South and Central Asia. The economic factors play a crucial role in shaping India's policy in Central Asia.

The study of *India's economic diplomacy Central Asian* countries by Mavlanov (2013)[46] explained that economic diplomacy of India in CARs have potential in investment and growing consumer market, additionally having great significance for wholly owned and joint ventures, that could benefit both sides. Besides CARs is an imperative for India in the execution of transport and communication infrastructure that would connect this region with the world market. Author highlights the energy resources in this region are not transported in an efficient way. Therefore, development of pipeline infrastructure and exploration of untapped resources open up prospects for their geological exploration, production, processing and transportation. Thus, India could swiftly develop cooperation in all these areas. On the other hand, author discusses that India could avail multilateral diplomacy with the international cooperation of Central Asian region and SCO, by means of old and new models of inter-regional economic cooperation in Central and South Asia.

Customs Union and Eurasian Union: Implication for India by Patnaik (2013)[47] discuses that after independence of CARs have diversify their trade links nevertheless the demand of their products does not crop up outside the former Soviet Union, with the exception of natural resources. Consequently,

---

[46]   I. Mavlanov. (2013). 'India's Economic Diplomacy in Central Asia: A New Architecture of Interregional Cooperation'. *In:* R. Malhotra, P. L. Dash, and S. Gill. (eds.), *South and Central Asia: Quest for Peace and Cooperation*. Chandigarh: Centre for Research in Rural and Industrial Development, pp. 165-172.

[47]   A. Patnaik. (2013). 'Customs Union and Eurasian Union: Implication for India'. *In:* R. Malhotra. S. Gill and N. Kumar (eds.), *Perspectives on Bilateral and Regional Cooperation: South and Central Asia*. Chandigarh: Centre for Research in Rural and Industrial Development, pp. 79-88.

Russia is a major trading partner of these nations. Therefore, Russia and newly independent states have to pursue very important option of creating a single economic space. However, both West and China have advanced their vision of "Revival of Silk Road". The revival of this road increase the significance of the CARs, because Central Asia would became a bridge between China-Europe trades. It would reduce the importance of Russia; as a result, Russia tries to maintain its monopoly through Eurasian integration. The Eurasian Economic Community (EURASEC) was the first stab to design a common economic space. Author highlights other effort of regional economic integration through Custom Union. In the study author explained that creating economic unions have very important implication for India, in the current scenario Central Asia is repeatedly referred as India's extended neighbourhood. Thus, India plays active role in its neighbouring countries in general and particularly in Afghanistan and Central Asia. For enhancing India's economic relations with CARs, India has reduced its trade barriers through entering into regional cooperation of this region. For that reason Eurasian and Custom Union provides opportunity for India.

India's Role and Interest in Central Asia by Capmbell (2013)[48] reveals that India's geopolitical strategy is in developing strong relations with Central Asian republics, specifically to meet its energy requirements and to address the security challenges. Nevertheless, India's experiences in this region from last decade and so is indicative of various challenges, including the China's increasing hold in Central Asia. In this connection many analysts' offer different opinions regarding India's presence in Central Asia, wherein it is obvious that India has yet to translate the aspirations of it's Connect Central Asia policy into strategic actions in order to achieve the position that its neighbors have already maintained. India's "…discursive activity by far exceeds the reality of bilateral relationships" however, as we approach 2014, India needs to established itself as a regional player, particularly to counter the increasing presence of China in Central Asia, which currently constitutes a big challenge to India.

---

[48] I. Campbell. (2013). India's Role and Interests in Central Asia. London: Saferworld, Available online at www.saferworld.org.uk (accessed on 13 July 2012).

Having constructed a wide ranging review and analysis of the literature concerning India-Central Asia relations in general and trade relations in particular, it seems plausible to argue that Central Asian republics stand as an important avenue for meeting the geopolitical and energy demands for India. Nonetheless, looking critically into the analysis that have been offered by various authors, vis-a-vie the theme under study, we are witness to a very selective kind of studies, wherein most of the authors have focussed either on the energy security, problems of connectivity or emerging role of major powers in this Central Asia region. Keeping all this in consideration, the present study seeks to proffer an inclusive analysis and understanding of the India-Central Asia bilateral relations not only in terms of energy agreements rather including business, trade and investment. For that reason, our methodological strategy have been of a mixed type, comprising of gravity model and revealed comparative advantage index (see chapter 1).

CHAPTER 3

Policy and Barriers of International Trade in India and Central Asian States

The economic theories emphasis that trade liberalization positively affects economic growth and development. By and large, these theories disagree with inward oriented economy. As shown in earlier chapters, a number of empirical studies have examined the direct relation between economic growth and openness of economy. International institutions such as the World Bank, the IMF and the OECD frequently advise that openness play vital role for the growth of the economy of any country.

Specifically, classical trade theories stress that the country's overall gain (economic growth) is based on comparative cost advantage and free trade of exports and imports, which consequently increases the welfare of the country. Indeed contemporarily, economists as Lucas (1988), Romer (1992), Barro and Sala-I-Martin (1995) analyze that openness impacts positively on economic growth. Similarly, Krueger (1998) empirically identifies that performance of growth and outer- oriented economy are directly related. Stiglitz (1998) shows that indicators of open economy such as trade/GDP ratio or average tariff level or indices of price distortion are linked with per capita income growth. Frankel and Romer (1999) analyze the relation between income levels and openness and argues that if trade share increase by one percent it will raise two percent income level. Fischer (2000) reveals that the relation between the domestic economy and the world economy is only alternative way for countries to experience growth. Nowak and Felicitas (2003) study, empirically based on cross-section approach indicates that trade policy impacts positively on economic growth. More recently, Bulent (2012) examine empirically the direct relation between trade openness and long-run economic growth for the sample period 1960-2000. However, in a sense some findings of his study though analyzing the same relation as discussed above however, indicate that several openness variables are considerably correlated with long-run economic growth.

The openness of economy is not without predicaments taking into account some of the empirical studies such as Dollar (1992), Sachs and Warner (1995), Edwards (1998) and Arnold (2006). These studies hold that high tariffs and trade restriction adversely affects long-term growth of income and it affects negatively on potential of the economy. Schularick and Solomou (2009) are also suggesting that high tariffs adversely affect the economic growth of a country.

Thus, in one or other way all these (above) studies suggest that international trade maximises the output and benefits all. Usually, all countries involved in international trade impose some restrictions on the free movements of goods and services. These restrictions and regulations which are generally known as trade or commercial policies, deal with the country's trade and commerce. In this chapter, an attempt has been made to briefly review the trade policies and other barriers of trade, which have been adopted by the India and Central Asian States. This will help us to prepare a framework for the scope, extent and focus of trade between India and CAR's.

India and Central Asian States

Like most developing countries, India and CAR's also pursued a development strategy based on import substitution industrialization in the early years of independence. As a part of this closed macro-economic policy, a protectionist trade policy regime and selective foreign direct investment policy has been evolved to encourage domestic industries. In such economic policies, a country cuts back on exports by imposing tariffs and by making competitive devaluation of its currency, which makes its own goods cheaper and while goods of the opposite trading country become expensive. However, as each country cut back on imports, it succeeded in exporting the economic downturn to its neighbours. This is known as beggar-thy-neighbour policy.[49] East Asian countries offer an example of this policy. These countries initiated a process of policy reforms wherein consequently they could increase their per capita income, reduced poverty, achieved universal literacy and sustained long-term growth. It is also known as East Asian Miracle. In the 1990s, specifically, this process of economic reforms was expedited in these countries and for more comprehensive changes in various areas of the economic sphere.

The economic reforms in India since 1991 have measurably coincided with economic changes in Central Asia. Since then both India and Central Asian Republics have speedily integrated with global economy. India nevertheless commenced to open-up trade and investment, right-on when Central Asian States achieved their independence i.e., around the late 1980s. These reform initiatives included, among other things: reducing the level and dispersion of tariffs and lowering other quantitative restrictions as well as streamlining regulations on domestic and foreign investments. These changes were instituted to accommodate the interests of domestic entrepreneurs and foreign investors and to bring dynamism to the economy.

The policies of speedy economic liberalization made the economies of Central Asia States and India more open and market managed. As a result, trade relation between the two has also changed. Economic reforms in the two regions brought fundamental changes in the pattern and direction of economic exchanges between them. With transformations in economies and external sector, the traditional age-old relationship in these neighbouring countries assumed new dimensions. It was marked by the adoption of economic reforms as a part of which a significant emphasis was laid on the process of liberalization particularly in the trade and investment regimes to intensify their integration with the world economy.

---

[49] Joseph Stiglitz (2002). The East Asia Crisis, *in Globalization and its Discontents*. New Delhi: Penguin Books, p. 107.

Policy Reforms in Central Asian States

Before the disintegration of Soviet Union, Central Asian States had no experience in conducting foreign trade, trade institutions and entire economic activities were handled by Moscow. Trade policies of centrally planned economy of Former Soviet Union (FSU) were highly inward-oriented and emphasized on self-sufficiency and self-reliance. Foreign trade was regarded as a "necessary evil" to obtain goods and services which could not be produced domestically. Industry enjoyed complete protection from international competition. State had also imposed an arbitrary specialization on the economy. As a result, efficient allocation of resources, which is the main advantage of free trade was not allowed to work. Central authority had to decide about the types and amounts of products to be imported to finance the material balance, but it had also to decide about the goods to be exported. Foreign trade was also characterized by quantitative restriction, exchange controls including bans on imports as well as exports. Whatever foreign trade was allowed, it was exclusively carried out by state-owned agencies and designated state-owned enterprises.

Inward-orientation of Soviet economy was sustained by huge size of the country and the formation of Council for Mutual Economic Assistance (CMEA), which included Socialist countries of Eastern Europe, Cuba and USSR. Soviet Union was highly integrated with CMEA countries. During mid 1980s, it alone accounted for more than two-third of CMEA imports. The commodity composition of trade with CMEA was that USSR exported fuels and raw materials in exchange for consumer goods and grocery products mostly from the East European countries of CMEA. Trade patterns based on ideological and political consideration were characterized by absurd specialization, uncertain reciprocal supplies of goods and high degree of integration imposed by the central planning.

International trade outside CMEA, particularly with Western European countries was very limited as it was viewed with suspicion. Trade with these countries was confined to importation of technological inputs and components needed for the development of heavy industry and space research. In order to facilitate these imports, exports of raw materials, minerals and metals including gold were allowed. The commodity composition, which USSR exported to these countries, remained limited in availability and low in quality. The situation became very fragile in 1980s when there was no growth in the Soviet hard currency exports (except energy). This led to a significant decline in imports in general and technology imports in particular, which were crucially needed to modernise the Soviet economy.

After the disintegration of USSR, the five Central Asian Countries: Kazakhstan, Kyrgyzstan, Turkmenistan, Tajikistan and Uzbekistan were trying to transform their economies. These countries follow different strategies to cope with the challenges to transform their economies. As a result, the outcomes also differ. Even with a quick view at the vast literature on transform, one can find early and late reforms as well as radical and gradualist reforms in Central Asia. Uzbekistan adopted a gradual and cautious approach to market reforms. While Kazakhstan and Kyrgyzstan followed a relatively more regressive approach. Turkmenistan and Tajikistan have cautiously joined the latter. These different policies have led to different macro-economic outcomes as well as different policy environments.[50]

Among the Central Asian States, Kazakhstan alone was as an integral part of the national economic complex of the former USSR, because it was endowed with unique rich minerals resources. Kazakhstan, therefore actively participated in the foreign trade of the former Soviet Union. Indeed, it occupied one of the pleading places in the USSR in terms of the volume of exports for a number of goods-nonferrous metals, ferrous-alloys, chromate ore and phosphorous. In the 1980s, more than 180 Kazakh enterprises were active in producing goods for export. Its array of export goods included about 200 items; the geographical destination for these goods included eighty countries around the world, with about 60 percent of the volume of export going to countries in the Council of Mutual Economic Assistance (CMEA).[51]

---

[50]   G. Sacdeva. (2005). 'Central Asian Economic Transformation and Indian Response'. *In:* V. Nagendra Rao and Mohammad Monir Alam (eds.), *Central Asia: Present Challenges and Future Prospects.* New Delhi: Knowledge World, p. 283.

[51]   M. Khasanova. (1998). 'Kazakhstan: Foreign Trade Policy'. *In:* Boris Rumer and Stanislav Zhukov (eds.), *Central Asia: The challenge of Independence.* New York: M.P. Sharpe, p. 169.

Still, all these states faced two major economic shocks: transition from central planning to market economy and consequent hyperinflation.[52] Trade and transit were interrupted with the formation of new borders, increased cost of production, which led to output decline and collapse of traditional markets. Industrial and agricultural production decreased due to disruption in access to inputs and market. The industries that Moscow had placed in CAR's had operated only by the grace of financial subsidies from the Centre, not on their own.[53] The CAR's in the initial stage of their transformation have thus displayed some common trends and many significant variations.

In each of the Central Asian Republics, the trade policy being currently followed, constitutes an integral part of a market- oriented economic system. An assessment of the trade policy from 1992 until early 1996 shows that except in Kyrgyzstan, which adopted a more liberal trading system and moved towards current account convertibility, whereas trade liberalization has been moderate in Kazakhstan. As a result, the performance in other states has been slow and uneven. Import restrictions from countries outside the states of former Soviet Union have been subject to various restriction including bans, licenses and high import duties. Export restriction in the form of licenses, quotas, state orders, tariffs and high surrender requirement of hard currency earnings have been the main barriers to trade liberalization. Trade has also been dominated by the state trading organization. Besides, barter and clearing arrangement reflecting shortage of foreign exchange, agricultural protectionism and lack of a simplified trade policy have also played a negative role.[54]

Of relatively recently Kyrgyzstan, Kazakhstan and Tajikistan have achieved significant progress in formulation of economic reforms such as in liberalizing imports and exports and fully convertibility of current account. However,

---

[52] R. Pomfret. (2006). 'Economic Growth Performance since Independence'. *In: The Central Asian Economies since Independence*. US: Princeton University Press, p. 5.

[53] B. Rumer. (1996). 'Disintegration and Reintegration in Central Asia: Dynamics and Prospects'. *In: Central Asia in Transition: Dilemmas of Political and Economic Development*. New York: M. E. Sharpe, p. 55.

[54] S. Zhukov. (2000). 'Foreign Trade and Investment'. *In:* Boris Rumer (eds.), *Central Asia and the New Global Economy*. New York: M. E. Sharpe, p.174.

Turkmenistan and Uzbekistan are still with limited improvement in trade policy and current account is not fully convertible.

The national currency of Kyrgyzstan is full convertible in current and capital accounts. It imposes simple average tariff 4.5 percent on imports to non-CIS countries and goods imported from CIS countries are duty free. The export licenses are required for weapons and military equipments, nuclear materials and drugs. Overall, the simple average tariff in Kyrgyzstan remains constant with small change, 4.8 percent in 2007 and 4.6 percent in 2009 and same 4.6 percent in 2011. Similarly, the case of duty free remains same from 2007 to 2011 as shown in table 3.1. However, in case of maximum duty, it falls from 250 in 2007 to 170 in 2009 to 160 in 2011. Same is the case of coefficient of variation, which declined from 126 in 2007 to 109 in 2011. Subsequently, number of tariff lines decreased from 11166 in 2007 to 10953 in 2009, but in 2011, it increased to 10989.

Equally, Kazakhstan liberalized its foreign trade and its national currency is convertible for transaction. In 1992-1993, the government of the republic of Kazakhstan adopted resolution determining measures on non-tariff regulation of foreign trade. These measures included the establishment of quotas and an export license system for export of strategically important raw materials. The system of export licenses and quotas covered 200 different commodity items, including metals, foodstuffs, grain and other consumer, industrial and construction materials.

From 1993 onwards most imports into the republic have been free from quotas, with a restricted range of imports-industrial waste, fertilizers, pestsides and herbicides for agriculture, diamond and jewellery and some kind of medicine, subject of licensing. This list was slightly changed in 1994; import licenses for diamond and jewellery were no longer required but had become necessary for baby food and explosive. At that time, the system of licensing was not so much aimed at import restriction per se as to the protection of health and life of the people.[55]

Goods imported for short-term use in Kazakhstan under the temporary import regime can be fully or partially exempt from duties, tax and non-tariff

---

[55]   M. Khasanova. (1998). *Op cit.*, p. 172.

regulations. The government has the right to issue a list of goods that can't be temporally imported to Kazakhstan. Goods not eligible for duty exemptions have traditionally included food products, industrial wastes and consumables. Similar to the 1994 foreign investment law, the law on investments, enacted in January 2003, provides custom duty exemption for import equipment and spare parts, if Kazakhstan produced stocks are unavailable or not of international standards.[56]

The Kazakhstan liberalises its economy that offers the most attractive business and investment climate among the countries in the CIS. Thus, the country has eliminated state intervention in the economy. This is why foreign countries are focusing in the economy of Kazakhstan, which has to some extent contributed to the economic growth. In this respect, reducing average tariff rates has been one of the key factors as evidenced from the following table 3.1, which reveals that tariff rates have gone down from 7.32 in 1995-99 to 4.1 in 2005-09 (WTO, Various Tariff Profiles).

Taking into account the scenario of Tajikistan, in 1996 state eliminated control over cereals, aluminium and cotton and abrogated the preconditions that exporters exchange some good portions of their hard currency earnings in order to increase the demand of national currency. Thus, it became perquisite for exporters to repatriate their hard currency earnings and commodities including cement, fruits and vegetables, wool, cotton, tobacco, metals, leather etc. that can be sold abroad. Given this Tajikistan needs imports licenses for some commodities that can affects certain spheres like the cultural legacies of the nation. Moreover, certain licenses are also required for the import of commodities such as pesticides, natural gas and electricity. Equally, export licenses are needed for metals, bulldozers, construction equipments, tractors, petroleum and electricity.

Unlikely, Uzbekistan the most ambitious CAR's had the same features of economic system as during Soviet Union such as centralized economic system and a high degree of dependence on Central administration. Beginning in 1991, Uzbekistan adopted a gradual approach to the transition from communism, relying heavily on the use of state controls, trade and foreign

---

[56] *Ibid.,* p. 173.

exchange restrictions, and large public investments. The trade regime remains relatively restrictive, with several administrative measures aimed at suppressing domestic and external trade still in place. The gradualism strategy is based on:

- systematic and institutional transformation, elimination of monopoly policies and financial reforms,
- introduction of market mechanism for price formation and liberalization of prices,
- creation of competitive market,
- abolishing of all barriers of trade and
- macro-economic stabilization.

Uzbekistan constantly frameworks its economy towards an open economic system, which reflects from the following statement of President Islam Karimov: We begin with the incontrovertible fact that a market economy is free economy and that it bears an open character. Hence, the future of Uzbekistan's economy is seen in its integration with the world economy.[57] The government developed foreign economic activity due to the formation of Organizational-administrative structure, and established the ministry of foreign economic relations. Its main objective was as follows:

- formation and implementation of foreign economic policy and creation of mechanism to stimulate foreign trade
- creation of legal and economic conditions to develop foreign economic activity
- creation of an infrastructure of foreign economic relations, including information systems and transportation services
- proposals to expand exports and
- protect both domestic and foreign participants of economic activity.

---

[57]   A. Isadjanov. (1998). 'The Role of Foreign Economic Activity-Past Experience and Problems of Future Development'. *In: Economic Reforms in Uzbekistan: characteristics and Responses.* Tokyo: The Sasakawa Peace Foundation, p. 46.

As for as Turkmenistan is concerned, it created the material base to establish Turkmenistan model for development, that was based on earlier structure. It chooses its own path of development. The president, Saparmurat Niazov said that, "we do not have need of revolution, we are for evolution."

Turkmenistan stabilizes its economy and in 1996, they change the structure of their economy as follows:

- create legal base for transform of economy
- structural transformation of economy
- implement institutional changes
- introduce own national currency and banking system
- process of privatization

The objective of structural transformation was to increase country's participation in international division of labour. Government encourages manufacturing products, channelling investment into social overhead capital and into the basic sectors of the economy. Government also stressed to enhance the country's trade potential. Subsequently, Turkmenistan's import policy was in favour of acquisition of advanced technology and equipments.

More or less, the five Central Asian Republics are having open economic systems, having high trade/GDP ratios except Turkmenistan and Uzbekistan, which have adopted inward oriented strategy. The initial trade relations were oriented towards CIS countries, because of existed infrastructure and old links. The CAR's diversify foreign trade after 1996 outside the Soviet area, although connectivity of foreign trade remains continued with Russia. In 1990's CAR's singed many regional trade agreements and Kyrgyzstan became member of WTO in 1998. Similarly, Kazakhstan has adopted liberal trade policy from 1996, the export duties were removed and simple average tariff on imports decreased to 12 percent, which further decreased to 8 percent in 2002. However, Uzbekistan's tariff schedule in 1995 at average level was 8 percent and then increased to 15.4 percent in 2010, similarly both Turkmenistan and Tajikistan impose protective tariff in addition with imposing export restrictions.

Table 3.1: Summary Indicators of MFN Tariff in Central Asian States

Country	Simple Average	Duty Free	Number of ad-valorem	Duties > 15 %	Duties > 15%	Maximum Duty	Coefficient of Variation	No. of Tariff lines
2011 Year of MFN Applied								
Kazakhstan	9.6	15.2	13.1	10.2	1.7	354	154	11234
Kyrgyzstan	4.6	48.8	0.4	0.4	2.0	160	109	10989
Tajikistan	7.8	1.5	0.5	0.4	0.3	335	80	13802
2010 Year of MFN Applied								
Kazakhstan	9.2	16.5	12.5	10.0	1.5	321	123	11171
Kyrgyzstan	4.6	48.7	0.4	0.4	0.2	166	110	10938
Tajikistan	7.8	1.0	0.5	0.3	2.3	170	124	11359
Uzbekistan	15.4	3.2	5.8	33.7	0.4	287	80	10984
2009 Year of MFN Applied								
Kazakhstan	5.9	23.4	8.5	3.2	3.0	332	127	10851
Kyrgyzstan	4.6	48.2	0.4	0.4	2.0	170	108	10953
Tajikistan	7.9	1.1	0.5	0.4	0.3	332	82	11176
Uzbekistan	15.9	3.2	5.8	33.7	0.8	487	102	10985
2008 Year of MFN Applied								
Kazakhstan	6.0	24.1	8.5	3.6	3.2	456	155	11078
Kyrgyzstan	4.7	48.2	0.3	0.4	2.1	195	111	10954
Tajikistan	-	-	-	-	-	-	-	-
Uzbekistan	15.5	1.3	4.5	33.4	0.3	522	81	10986
2007 Year of MFN Applied								
Kazakhstan	7.8	19.5	8.4	7.9	1.7	415	111	11199
Kyrgyzstan	4.8	47.2	0.3	0.2	1.9	250	126	11166
Tajikistan	7.9	1.0	0.5	0.3	0.3	429	102	10613
Uzbekistan	15.6	1.3	4.4	33.9	0.3	184	74	10610

Source: *World Trade Organization 2012.*

The simple average MFN tariff and trade weighted applied tariff of 2010 are shown in fig. 3.1. In Central Asian States, trade policies are not restrictive. The case of Uzbekistan is exception that has high trade barriers, but these barriers are uncommonly applied (ADB 2012). Both simple average MFN tariff and trade weighted applied tariff are low in Kyrgyzstan which stands respectively at 3.3 and 2.3 as of 2010.

Fig. 3.1:   Import Tariffs in Central Asian States

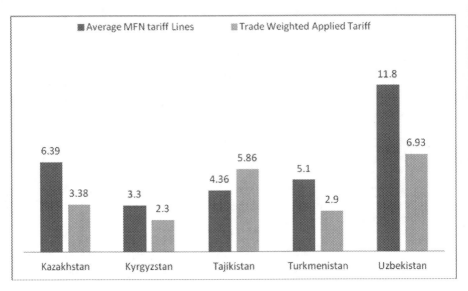

Source: World Bank (2012).

All Central Asian republics are open economies except Turkmenistan and Uzbekistan, which has restrictive barriers to trade. These republics as mentioned earlier adopted restrictive trade policies, because they have natural comparative advantage in gas and cotton (ADB 2012). However, Kyrgyzstan and Tajikistan economies are landlocked and their international trade is minimal but both economies are open in terms of adopting low restricting trade barriers. The oil boom in Kazakhstan and high world price of oil stimulate the Kazakhstan's international trade

To scrutinize trade policy in CAR's, several economic indicators related to trade are considered to analyze the strategy of trade policy such as per capita-GDP, openness of trade (imports+exports/GDP), corruption and economic freedom given in below table 3.2.

Table 3.2: Selected Economic Indicators

Indicators	Kazakhstan	Kyrgyzstan	Tajikistan	Turkmenistan	Uzbekistan
PCI-GDP	12015	2200	1923	6805	3048
Trade/GDP Ratio	0.77	1.43	0.43	1.23	0.59
Corruption Perception Index	133	154	157	170	170
Economic Freedom Index	68	89	131	169	162

1 Gross Domestic Product Per Capita ($ US, PPP) 2011. *Source: World Development Indicators, 2012.*

2 Openness to Trade, *Source: World Bank.*

As shown in above table, the per capita GDP ratio of Kazakhstan is high because of its heavily being rely on export of oil. Similarly, Tajikistan's per capita GDP ratio relies on exports of cotton and aluminum. While Turkmenistan's per capita GDP is heavily depended on export of natural gas and cotton. However, per capita GDP of Uzbekistan is nearly half that of Turkmenistan, with export earnings mostly relying on cotton and natural gas. Kyrgyzstan's per capita GDP is to some extent higher than Tajikistan and gain most of its export earnings from gold and hydropower.

Trade/GDP ratio is another measure to calculate the openness of economy of any country. It shows contribution of international trade in economy of the country. Among Central Asia republics, Kyrgyzstan and Turkmenistan shows high ratios of openness to trade standing at 1.43 and 1.23 respectively. On the other hand, corruption significantly obstructs trade. It increases cost and increases ambiguity in customs and tax. Central Asian republics experienced higher transportation cost within region and outside region (Raballand 2005). The Corruption Perception Index places Turkmenistan and Uzbekistan (170 out of 180) and for Tajikistan (157 out of 180), Kyrgyzstan (154 out of 180) at high level, but Kazakhstan's index is low as compared to other Central Asian States i.e., 133 out of 180.

Yet another variable to openness of trade is the Economic Freedom Index (EFI), which influences international trade performance. The Heritage Foundation uses Economic Freedom Index to calculate economic freedom that includes open competition, tariff and non-tariff barriers and non-discrimination (Miller and Kim, 2010). In this perspective, EFI has high relevance in Central Asia. Classifying CARs as per this index, Kazakhstan and Kyrgyzstan are moderately free, whilst Tajikistan is mostly un-free. Uzbekistan and Turkmenistan are repressed (Heritage Foundation, 2012).

The inadequate development and meager infrastructure and trade facilitation are still other determining factors for international trade. These factors are included in Logistics Performance Index (LPI) of World Bank. The LPI is designed and implemented by World Bank International Trade and Transport Department with Tuku School of Economics (Finland). According to indices of LPI, Central Asian countries have poor quality of trade and transport infrastructure.

Table 3.3: Logistic Performance Index of Central Asian States (2012)

Indicators		Kazakhstan	Uzbekistan	Kyrgyzstan	Tajikistan
LPI Rank	Rank	86	117	130	136
	Lower Bound	61	61	107	105
	Upper Bound	118	153	144	151
LPI Score	Score	2.69	2.46	2.35	2.28
	Lower Bound	2.46	2	2.18	2.02
	Upper Bound	2.93	2.93	2.52	2.53
Percentage of Highest Performance		54.2	46	43.3	41.1
Customs	Rank	73	118	84	85
	Score	2.58	2.25	2.45	2.43
Infrastructure	Rank	79	120	90	138
	Score	2.6	2.25	2.49	2.03
International Shipment	Rank	92	127	147	135
	Score	2.67	2.38	2	2.33
Logistics quality & Competence	Rank	74	117	129	130
	score	2.75	2.39	2.25	2.22
Tracing & Tracking	Rank	70	105	132	143
	score	2.83	2.53	2.31	2.13

Timelines	Rank	132	101	135	146
	Score	2.73	2.96	2.69	2.51

Source: *World Bank 2012.*

In general Central Asian countries do not fare well on the majority of the indices. Key barriers for trade for these for these countries are associated with the inadequate quality of trade, transport infrastructure, underdeveloped logistic services as well as inefficient custom clearance process (table 3.3). However, LPI value indicates that all the countries of this region and in particular, Kazakhstan and Uzbekistan achieved visible progress. Indeed most important according to the LPI, were improvements in rankings for timeliness of international shipments and infrastructure. The more improvement requires huge investment into energy and transport infrastructure, as well as to develop infrastructure and construction of oil and gas line pipelines. The Central Asian countries gain significantly because of bettering trade facilitation.[58]

In Central Asia, all oil-exporting countries are heavily depending on exporting energy products and metals and non-oil exporting countries are depending on energy imports. That is why fluctuation in international prices of energy and metal products affects Central Asian economy.

---

[58] Felipe and Kumar (2010). *The Role of Trade Facilitation in Central Asia: A Gravity Model.* Levy Economics Institute of Bard College, Working Paper No. 628.

Fig. 3.2: Net Barter Terms of Trade Index

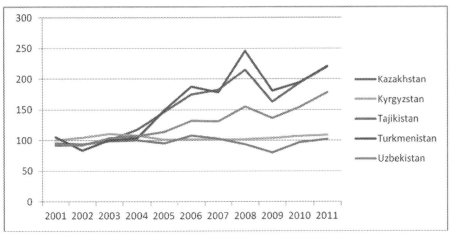

Source: World Bank.

The figure 3.2 indicates that Kazakhstan, Turkmenistan and Uzbekistan are net exporters, experienced progress in terms of trade measured by net barter terms of trade index. Kyrgyzstan due to increases in fuel prices, experienced high price for export commodities. However, in Tajikistan higher prices of imported energy products results in worsening the nation's terms of trade.

Policy Reforms in India

The trade policy of India was inward-oriented and high protectionist before 1990s. The objective of this strategy was to protect infant industry from foreign competition. The various policy instruments to protect domestic economy were mainly licenses policy for industries, reservation of goods for public sectors and private sectors, tariff and non-tariff barriers and so on. Therefore, until the late 1980s Indian economy remained closed, due to this foreign exchange reserve of India decline. To manage economic imbalance consequent upon the import substitution and protectionist policy, India adopt liberalization policy that improved trade- ratio (Raut 2003 and Shinde, 2010). The main objective of India's foreign Trade Policy 2004-09 was to double global trade share by 2009 in addition to decline transaction costs, establish special economic zones for export promotion and important objective of this policy was to enhance economic integration of the Indian economy with world economy.

After the introduction of economic reforms and liberalization in 1991 with focus on external sector, directions of trade policies were changed such as tariff protection decreased, relaxation in import and industrial licenses regime. Additionally in 1994, amended copyright law under the Trade Related Intellectual Property Rights (TRIPs) agreement further revamped this sphere. Tariff rates were reduced to 150 percent from 300 percent. Simultaneously custom duty rates were also brought down.

Fig. 3.3:   Un-weighted Average Tariff of India (1996- 2009)

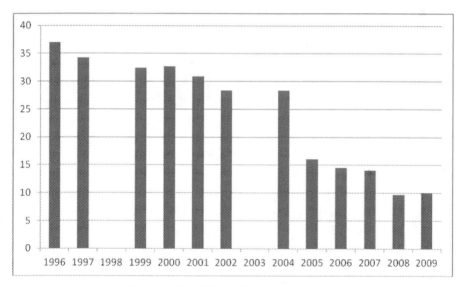

Source: World Trade Organization 2012.

Tariffs and quantitative restrictions were removed for capital goods as well as for intermediate goods. The tariff level reduced from 81.8 percent in 1990 to 37 percent in 1996, but it increased in 2000 due to introduction of specific tariff for the protection of garment products and textile fabric. Subsequently tariff rate continuously decreases to 10.1 percent as of 2009 (Fig 3.3). However, tariff reduction procedure again declined in 2002 on the removal of import licenses. The tariff imposed on three omissions as shown in fig. 3.4. All tariff lines reduced from 19.2 percent in 2005 to 12.9 percent in 2009, but for agriculture goods tariff level to some extent remained constant. Tariff level on industrial goods were also reduced from 16.6 percent in 2005 to 10.3 percent in 2009.

Fig. 3.4: Trends in Average Tariff (2005-2009).

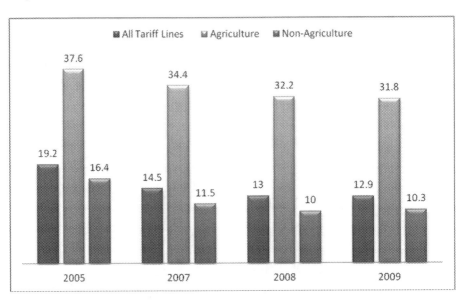

Source: World Trade Organization 2012.

The tariffs on agriculture products (like livestock and livestock products, fishers and dairy products) were not included in a new tariff reduction programme. Tariff on agricultural products reduced from 37.6 percent in 2005 to 31.8 percent in 2009. Tariff rate on different agriculture products are higher than industrial products as shown in table 3.4.

Table 3.4: Tariff on Processed Food Products

Product Group	2007	2008	2009
Animal Products	31.6	31.6	33.1
Dairy Products	34.5	33.8	33.7
Fruits, Vegetables, Plants	30.8	29.7	30.4
Coffee, Tea	55.9	56.1	56.3
Cereals & Preparation	31.1	30.8	32.2

Oilseeds, fats & oil	48.8	26.2	18.2
Sugar & confectionary	34.4	34.4	34.4
Fish &fish products	29.6	29.6	29.8
Cotton	17.0	17.0	12.0
Other agriculture products	22.0	21.9	21.7

Source: *World Trade Organization.*

India maintained monopolies on all food grains apart from barley and maize, and in case of crude sunflower and sunflower oil, mustard oil and refined rape, tariffs rate are used against foreign competition. Nonetheless, domestic prices of several agricultural commodities including food grains and sugar were same as world prices. The import licenses were withdrawn on textiles and garments in 2001. As a result, some specific duties were imposed in favour of these products.

The rationalization of tariff structure occurred and progress was made towards achieving a degree of uniformity and removing some tariff anomalies. Simple average tariff decreases from 14.5 percent to 12.6 percent in 2011. However, coefficient of variation and number of tariff lines shown nearly the same trend from 2007 to 20011 (Table 3.5).

Table 3.5: Indicators of Tariff in India

All Products					
Indicators	**2007**	**2008**	**2009**	**2010**	**2011**
Simple Average	14.5	7.5	12.9	13.0	12.6
Duty free	3.9	6.5	2.8	2.8	3.5
Non-ad valorem	5.0	6.0	5.2	5.2	5.0
Duties >15	21.6	17.3	17.1	16.6	16.5
Duties >3 AVG	2.5	2.7	2.1	2.3	2.3
Maximum duty	268	150	246	170	315
Coefficient of Variation	91	125	123	124	119
Number of MFN applied tariff lines	11693	11893	11360	11359	11377

Source: *World Trade Organization.*

The country's volume of trade not only depends on trade but other indicators are equally responsible such as transport cost, economic freedom index, and infrastructure and corruption perception index. As for India's economic freedom is concerned its rank is 119th and trade freedom score is 63.6 in 2013 index. Its score is increasing from last many years such as 38 in 2005, due to progress in the management of public finance. India's inadequate institutional infrastructure retards the long-term economic development. Additionally, with meagre legal and regulatory framework, corruption is becoming a serious problem throughout economy. India's freedom from corruption rank increased from 84 in 2011 to 93 in 2013 (heritage foundation).

The Trade freedom Index (absence of tariff and non-tariff barriers) shows the score of India has increased from 24.0 in 2006 to 51.2 in 2007, which further increased to 63.6 in 2013. Similarly, in case of investment freedom index, the rank has increased from 97 in 2007 to 130 in 2013. However, the most important indicator of openness is trade/GDP ratio, which also shows that India is stressing on external sector. The trade/GDP ratio as shown in table 3.6 indicates that contribution of trade in GDP is increasing from the last few years.

Table 3.6: India's Logistic Performance Index

2012 LPI			2010 LPI			2007 LPI		
LPI rank	LPI score	% of highest performer	LPI rank	LPI score	% of highest performer	LPI rank	LPI score	% of highest performer
46	3.08	66.4	47	3.12	67.9	39	3.07	64.9

Source: World Bank, Database

Equally, LPI measures are recognized as the essence for trade and growth. The LPI compares logistics performance of 155 countries on a scale of 1 to 5, 1 for worst and 5 for best. Overall improvement in LPI and trade facilitation stimulates trade and export diversification and creates favourable environment for foreign direct investment. According to World Bank's LPI, India's rank fell from 39th in 2007 to 46th in 2012, the drop in rank could negatively affect foreign investment. The situation of score is same as rank. In 2007, LPI score was 3.06 and in 2012 score was 3.08. The overall performance of LPI of India is better than its neighbouring countries except China.

Table 3.7: Logistic Performance Index of India (2012)

Indicators		Values
LPI Rank	Rank	46
	Lower Bound	44
	Upper Bound	53
LPI Score	Score	3.08
	Lower Bound	3.0
	Upper Bound	3.15
% of highest performance		66.4
Customs	Rank	52
	Score	2.77
Infrastructure	Rank	56
	Score	2.87
International Shipment	Rank	54
	Score	2.98
Logistics quality & Competence	Rank	38
	score	3.14
Tracing & Tracking	Rank	54
	score	3.09
Timelines	Rank	44
	Score	3.58

Source: *World Bank*

The terms of trade, measure gain or loss due to comparative change in exports and imports price. Figure 3.5 indicates that India's net barter terms of trade is increasing at increasing rate except for the year 2011. In 2005, India's net barter terms of trade was 105.2, in 2008 it increased to 117.2. The average percentage growth rate from 2005 to 2008 was 3 percent. Nevertheless, in

2009 it significantly jumped to 131.7 to 138.5 in 2010. However, its terms of trade declined nearly to 2 percent in 2011.

Fig. 3.5: India's Net Barter Terms of Trade

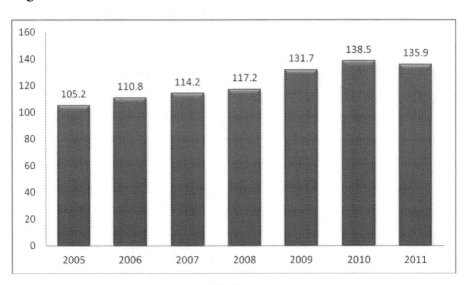

Source: *World Bank 2012.*

Overall, Indian economy has persistent growth and focus on industrial development that stimulated the demand for advanced technology and capital-intensive products. Due to this industrial sector and export-oriented economy enhanced, however domestic resources are scarce as a result Indian economy is more depend on foreign inputs. The growing demand of imported inputs increases import prices. This is basic cause of deterioration of India's net barter terms of trade.

From the whole discussion, it is implied that both India and Central Asian States lacks strategic focus and mainly emphasized on protecting domestic market from foreign competition. In addition, with poor logistic infrastructure, landlocked and physical landscapes are barriers of connecting CAR's with India. To reduce the negative aspects of geographic location, these countries could gain from increasing trade relations with neighbouring countries; reduce tariffs and non-tariff restrictions and enhancing infrastructure.

CHAPTER 4

India and Central Asia: Trade Relations

Historically, India has strong relations with Central Asian States (Kazakhstan, Kyrgyzstan, Tajikistan, Turkmenistan and Uzbekistan). In the ancient times, both India and Central Asia were powerful centers with great deal of economic and cultural relations.[59] The ancient "Silk Route" connects India and Central Asian region due to which both have experienced the exchanges in cultural, political and economic spheres. However, during Soviet period economic relation between India and Central Asia were under control of Moscow. The USSR was major trading partner of India and first trade agreement was signed in 1953. Moreover, seven agreements were signed prior the disintegration of Soviet Union.[60] The trade was regulated under Rupee Trade System and non-convertible currencies. In addition, the Indo-Soviet economic relations were based on nature and character of India-Central Asia relations.[61] However, after

---

[59] I. Mavlonov. (2004). India's Economic Diplomacy with Central Asian Nations and the Economic Development of the Region. *Dialogue*, 7 (3): 24.

[60] G. Sachdeva. (2010). 'Regional Economic Linkages.' *In:* Nirmala Joshi (eds.), *Reconnecting India and Central Asia: Emerging Security and Economic Dimensions*. Washington DC and Sweden: Central Asia-Caucasus Institute Silk Road Studies Programme, p. 133.

[61] *Ibid.*, p.133.

collapse of Soviet Union, economic relation between India and Central Asia declined.

In the current global economic scenario this age-old relationship has attained greater significance. Despite the fact that present relationship between India and Central Asia is increasing but below the expected potential. The trade is confined to traditional commodities such as India mostly exports pharmaceuticals, tea, readymade garments, cotton yarn, jute manufactures etc to Central Asia and imports iron and steel, and fruits etc. from this region. The sustained economic growth in Central Asia, increasing foreign trade and foreign exchange reserves in addition with foreign investment inflow could provide opportunities for India to enhance economic relation with Central Asia.

India's Merchandise Trade with CAR's

The value of merchandise trade between India and CAR's region for the period from 2001-02 to 2012-13 has been presented in (Table 4.1). India's total trade with the CAR's region increased from US$ 114.05 million in 2000-01to $US 746.32 million in 2012-13. The significant increase in the total trade was mainly due to the development of diplomatic relation and signing many agreements. India however, experienced favourable balance of trade, as exports increased from US$ 83.33 in 2000-01 to US$ 551.2 million in 2012-13. On the other hand, India's imports from CAR's have also registered a sustained rise from US$ 30.72 million in 2000-01 to US$ 256.34 million in 2011-12. However, it showed an unlikely decrease to US$ 195.12 million in 2012-13.

The percentage growth of exports show a fluctuated trend and on an average shown 18-percent growth rate was recorded during the period. While as imports show several times decline growth rates, its growth rate decreased from 37.6 percent in 2002-03 to 15.6 percent in 2005-06. However, in 2006-07 imports growth rate increased to 98 percent, mainly due to India imported zinc articles from CARs, and in the following, a mixed trend is found.

Table 4.1: Values of India- CAR's Merchandise Trade, (2000-01 to 2012-13) ($ Million)

Year	Exports	Percentage growth of exports	Imports	Percentage growth of imports	Trade Balance	Trade Turnover	Percentage growth of total trade
2000-01	83.33		30.72		52.61	114.05	
2001-02	68.78	-31.22	28.50	-7.23	40.28	97.28	-14.70
2002-03	85.56	26.17	39.22	37.6	46.34	124.78	28.26
2003-04	151.83	77.45	50.79	29.50	101.04	202.62	62.4
2004-05	174.18	14.74	62.43	22.9	111.75	236.61	16.77
2005-06	168.47	-3.28	72.15	15.6	96.32	240.62	1.7
2006-07	191.40	13.61	142.87	98	48.53	334.27	38.92
2007-08	232.32	21.38	112.26	-21.42	120.06	344.58	3.08
2008-09	258.23	11.15	260.36	131.9	-2.13	518.59	50.50
2009-10	269.27	4.28	212.37	-18.43	56.9	481.64	-7.13
2010-11	302.83	12.5	192.99	-9.13	109.84	495.82	2.94
2011-12	429.55	41.84	256.34	32.83	173.21	685.89	38.33
2012-13	551.2	28.32	195.12	-23.9	356.08	746.32	8.81

Source: Ministry of Commerce, GOI.

India's export value of individual CAR's countries during 2000-01 to 2012-13 was presented in table 4.2. Among CAR's, India exports major portion to Kazakhstan, which accounted US$ 50.08 million in 2000-01 and US$ 244.39 million in 2011-12. However, Kyrgyzstan was second largest export destination of India's exports till 2005-06, but after this, Uzbekistan became the second largest trading partner in CAR's as shown in the table 4.2.

Table 4.2: India's Exports to CAR's, 2000-01 to 2012-13 ($US Million)

Year	Kazakhstan	Kyrgyzstan	Tajikistan	Turkmenistan	Uzbekistan
2000-01	50.08	17.59	3.55	2.71	9.39
2001-02	45.70	10.97	1.22	4.35	6.53
2002-03	46.88	14.67	8.65	10.29	5.08
2003-04	74.81	38.20	4.47	19.21	15.14
2004-05	81.42	49.57	6.59	15.26	21.35
2005-06	90.86	28.09	6.24	18.83	24.44
2006-07	83.18	37.08	7.46	33.99	29.69
2007-08	111.99	31.52	12.40	36.09	40.32
2008-09	131.68	22.92	16.71	41.40	45.53
2009-10	136.54	22.92	16.71	36.15	45.53
2010-11	172.16	25.79	18.31	26.16	60.42
2011-12	244.39	30.55	21.28	43.95	89.39
2012-13	286.23	34.99	35.16	69.92	124.90

Source: *Ministry of Commerce, GoI.*

The largest export products of India to CAR's were drugs, pharma and fine chemicals; these increased from US$ 24.21 million in 2000-03 to US$ 83.22 million in 2003-06. During 2009-12, it increased to US$ 308.01 million, accounting 31.10 percent in the total exports. Similarly, export of coffee, tea & spices increased from US$ 62.38 million during 2000-03, accounting 26.25 percent to US$ 135.98 million during 2009-12 followed by readymade of cotton and accessories (14.05 percent), drugs, pharma and fine chemicals (10.19 percent), and articles of leather (8.7 percent). However, during 2009-12, instead of coffee, tea and spices, drug, pharma and fine chemicals which earlier were at rank third, stood at top position with the percentage share 31.10 percent, followed by coffee, tea and spices (13.7 percent). Readymade cloths and accessories (12 percent) and nuclear reactors and boilers etc (7.8 percent). Among other things that India exports to the CAR's includes meat & preparation, electrical machinery and equipments, and transport equipments (Table 4.3).

Table 4.3: Composition of India's Exports to CAR's ($US Million)

Commodities	2000-03	2003-06	2006-09	2009-12
Meat & Preparation	0.20 (0.08)	9.57 (1.94)	18.9 (2.8)	29.63 (3.0)
Coffee, Tea & Spices	62.38 (26.25)	85.28 (17.25)	54.15 (7.9)	135.98 (13.7)
Drugs Pharma & fine chemicals	24.21 (10.19)	83.22 (16.8)	184.44 (27.04)	308.01 (31.10)
Articles of leather	20.75 (8.7)	22.07 (4.5)	17.73 (2.6)	15.66 (1.6)
Readymade of cotton & accessories	33.39 (14.05)	66.07 (13.4)	90 (13.2)	118.23 (12.0)
Cotton yarn fabrics madeups etc	14.01 (5.9)	73.86 (15.0)	44.6 (6.54)	58.34 (5.9)
Nuclear Reactors, & Boilers etc	15.05 (6.3)	45.51 (9.2)	65.1 (9.55)	77.18 (7.8)
Electrical Machinery & Equipments	4.18 (1.8)	25.85 (5.23)	55.86 (8.2)	74.08 (7.5)
Transport Equipments	1.33 (0.5)	2.23 (0.45)	5.02 (0.74)	20.56 (2.1)
Surgical products	3.04 (1.3)	4.94 (1.0)	11.13 (1.63)	23.56 (2.4)
Others	59.13 (24.9)	75.88 (15.34)	132.02 (19.36)	130.42 (13.2)

Note: Figures in parentheses shows percentage of total exports.
Source: *Ministry of Commerce, GOI.*

Among CARs, India imports major portion from Kazakhstan, and these imports increased from US$ 14.04 million in 2000-01 to US$ 166.35 million in 2011-12. Uzbekistan is second largest import source for India among CAR's, whose exports to India increased from US$ 10.58 million in 2000-01 to US$ 33.91 million in 2006-07 to US$ 61.58 million in 2011-12, followed by Turkmenistan, Tajikistan and Kyrgyzstan.

Table 4.4: India's Imports from CAR's ($ US Million)

Year	Kazakhstan	Kyrgyzstan	Tajikistan	Turkmenistan	Uzbekistan
2000-01	14.04	4.43	0.54	1.12	10.58
2001-02	7.39	0.56	1.34	1.95	17.27
2002-03	12.73	0.47	0.08	5.40	20.54
2003-04	9.26	0.54	3.95	9.34	27.70
2004-05	15.39	0.63	4.09	10.87	31.46
2005-06	26.30	1.47	5.89	12.35	26.13
2006-07	88.30	0.76	7.95	11.95	33.91
2007-08	76.78	0.91	9.81	8.55	16.20
2008-09	159.03	1.03	17.47	12.10	70.74
2009-10	154.91	0.64	16.85	10.00	29.97
2010-11	138.42	1.20	23.02	9.73	20.63
2011-12	191.86	0.89	7.09	19.46	37.04
2012-13	139.99	2.09	12.86	8.33	31.85

Source: *Ministry of Commerce, GOI.*

The table 4.5 presents the composition of India's import items from CARs. India imports limited number of items from CAR's such as zinc and articles, natural pearls, salt, sulphur and stones etc. and Iron, steel and aluminium were largest import items. However, in addition to these traditional items other new items have been added in imported basket of India from this region.

Table 4.5: Composition of India's Imports from CAR's ($US Million)

Commodities	2000-03	2003-06	2006-09	2009-12
Salt, Sulpher and stones etc	8.25 (8.4)	16.66 (9.00)	56.86 (11.03)	99.86 (15.1)
Organic & inorganic chemicals	2.00 (0.02)	3.16 (1.7)	14.35 (2.8)	44.15 (6.7)
Cotton	31.44 (32)	56.65 (30.6)	63.89 (12.4)	16.43 (2.49)
Natural pearls etc	13.00 (13.2)	9.86 (5.32)	20.44 (4.0)	111.78 (16.9)
Iron & Steel	8.00 (8.13)	26.34 (14.21)	83.78 (16.25)	83.11 (12.6)
Aluminum	2.08 (2.11)	2.16 (1.2)	29.16 (5.7)	45.56 (6.9)
Lead & articles	-	0.15 (0.08)	29.55 (5.7)	16.74 (2.53)
Zinc & articles thereof	15.00 (15.3)	52.76 (28.5)	191.99 (37.3)	149.11 (22.5)
Others	20.00 (20.3)	17.63 (9.5)	25.47 (5.0)	94.2 (14.2)

Note: Figures in parentheses shows percentage of total imports.

Source: *Ministry of Commerce, GOI*

The composition of India's imports from CAR's shows that Zinc & articles were largest import item, which increased from US$ 15 million in period 2000-03 to US$ 191 million in period 2006-09. Declining marginally during 2009-12 this item still tops the items imported from CAR's. The other imported item were natural pearls, which increased from US$ 9.86 million to US$ 111.78 million during 2003-06 and during 2009-12. It increased almost twelve times and constituting 16.9 percent of total export share in 2009-12. This is given in table 4.5.

India-Kazakhstan Relations

Indo-Kazakh trade is the most dynamic segment of India's foreign trade in Central Asian region. In February 1992, when president of Kazakhstan visited India, he considered India as an important trade partner in the region of south Asia. India was one of the first countries to support Nursultan Nazarbaev's idea to establish the Conference on the Interaction and Confidence Building Measures in Asia (CICA), which is a multi-national forum for enhancing cooperation towards promoting peace, security and stability in Asia.

Therefore, India and Kazakhstan have been in the process of developing good trade relation and both countries signed many agreements on trade. In 1994 Deputy Minister Commerce Mr. Salman Khurshed visited Kazakhstan and during his visit, an agreement was signed to establish joint ventures and business council (Appendix 1).

Subsequently, growing trade relations have led to very rapid development of economic relations. This has been evident in the growing volume of trade turnover and its diversification over the decade. Trade and Commerce are considered an important component of expanding multi-faceted partnership between India and Kazakhstan. Kazakhstan offers an enormous amount of opportunities for trade and investment and vice versa.[62] In recent years, there has been a significant promotion in export and import resulting in a huge total trade turnover as is evident from the data given in figure 4.1. The growing total trade turnover has generally been in favour of India. India's exports to Kazakhstan have increased substantially from US$ 50.08 million in 2000-01 to US$ 90.86 million in 2005-06 and further to US$ 244 million in 2011-12. Similarly, India's imports have also shown an increasing trend, which stands at US$ 14.04 million in 2000-01 to US$ 88.30 million in 2006-07 to US$ 166 million in 2011-12. By and large India has favourable trade balance with Kazakhstan, showing an increased trade surplus of US$ 36.04 million in 2000-01, US$ 66.03 in 2004-05 and US$ 78.04 in 2011-12. However, between 2006-09 trade balance was in favour of Kazakhstan with trade surplus

---

[62] M. Samir. (2012). India-Kazakhstan Strategic Partnership in the 21st Century. *Foreign Policy Research Centre*, 10 (2): 251.

accounting for US$ 27.35 million. India's trade with Kazakhstan during the last one decade commands a share of less than one per cent of the total India's international trade.

Fig. 4.1: India's Trade with Kazakhstan ($US million)

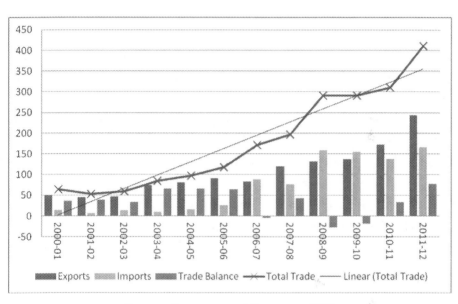

Source: Department of Commerce, GOI.

The rate of growth in India's trade with the Kazakhstan has been very impressive during 2000-01 to 2012-13, the trade between India and Kazakhstan has increased from US$ 133.42 million to US$ 426.22 million, which confirms that Kazakhstan continues to be the main trade partner of India in Central Asian region in terms of both exports and imports. A study of the range of commodities exchanged between the two countries can give a closer idea about the nature and composition of trade.

India's major export items to Kazakhstan were coffee and tea (HS 09), drugs, pharmaceutical and fine chemicals (HS 30) with share of (22 percent) and 18 percent respectively in 2011-12, followed by nuclear reactors etc (HS 85) (16 percent) and readymade cotton (HS 61) (14 percent). Natural and cultural (HS 71) and salt, sulphur and earth (HS 25) were major import items of India from Kazakhstan constituting 29 percent and 26 percent respectively in the period 2011-12, followed by Zinc and articles (HS 79) with a share of 22 percent.

The growing collective interests between India and Kazakhstan, and the identical views between them over a number of issues have led to very rapid development of economic relations, which is evident from the growing volume of trade turnover and its diversification. A close look at the yearly export commodity profile indicates that the share of traditional products, which constitute a large percentage of India's total exports declined while the share of non-traditional items almost doubled. The study of diversification of the commodity structure of Indian exports to the Kazakhstan has an obvious advantage in terms of growth of trade relations between India and Kazakhstan. This is evident by the fact that several new items have been added continuously through different trade agreements. India has an opportunity to concentrate on other economic niches in Kazakhstan. The growing need for chemical, mining, and electrical equipment, and IT and services. telecommunications and electronics, and the training of specialists in IT, healthcare, environmental technology, and tourism are areas were Indian expertise is strong and can play a significant role in developing these sectors in Kazakhstan.

India-Kyrgyzstan Relations

The economic relationships between India and Kyrgyzstan have been developed just after the establishment of diplomatic relations. The then president of the Kyrgyzstan Mr. Askar Akaev visited India in April 1999 and signed number of agreements like avoidance of double taxation, MoU on civil aviation matters and treaty on mutual legal assistance in criminal matters. In August 1999, the government of Kyrgyzstan invited Vice-President of India Mr. Krishan Kant as chief guest on Independence Day celebration. In 2002, Mr. Askar Akaev, president of Kyrgyzstan again visited India; and focused on bilateral and international issues including economic and political relations and Indian technical assistance (Appendix 2). Although the current level of trade is low with some specific traditional commodities being exchanged, but both nations are keen to enhance the economic and trade relationships in new areas with diversified commodities.

The trade between India and Kyrgyzstan have been with fluctuating trend in 2000-01 as clearly depicted in figure 4.2. The total trade has increased from US$ 22.02 million to US$ 50.2 million in 2004-05, and declined to US$ 29.56 million in 2005-06, but it increased to US$ 31.22 million in 2011-12. Similarly, India's exports to Kyrgyzstan increased from US$ 17.59 million in 2000-01 to US$ 49.57 million in 2004-05, and declined to US$ 28.09 million in 2005-06 and then to US$ 25.79 million in 2010-11. On the other hand, India's imports from Kyrgyzstan constitute a meagre amount accounting US$ 4.43 million in 2000-01, after which the value of imports did not increase more than US$ 1.47 million. India's exports are more than its imports with Kyrgyzstan; as a result India experiences surplus trade balance.

Fig. 4.2:   India's Trade with Kyrgyzstan.

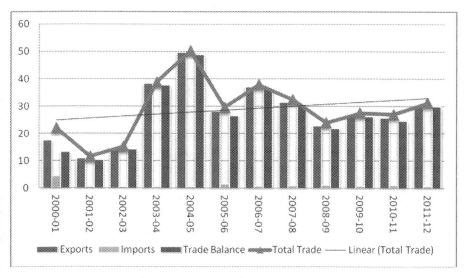

Source: Ministry of Commerce, GOI.

The major items of exports were readymade cotton garments (HS 61: US$ 9.42 million), readymade woollen garments (HS 62: US$ 6.29 million), pharmaceutical products (HS 30: US$ 5.65 million), coffee and tea (HS 09: US$ 1.75 million) and meat and preparation (HS 02: US$ 1.59 million) in the period 2011-12. Similarly, the major import items were inorganic chemicals (HS 28: $US 0.29 million), raw hides (HS 41: US$ 0.09 million), wool fine (HS 51: US$ 0.04 million), iron & steel (HS: US$ 0.08 million) and nuclear reactors and boilers (HS: US$ 0.03 million).

Indo-Kyrgyzstan has great significance for cooperation in various areas. In order to build up bilateral economic cooperation and trade, Indo-Kyrgyz Joint Commission on Trade and Economic, Science, Technical Cooperation, and the Joint Business Council have been formed.[63] In 1992, Indo-Kyrgyz commission was set up and subsequently several meetings were held and External Trade and Industry Minister Mr. Djienbekov prioritized several sectors in Kyrgyzstan where investment is viable for India such as information technology, food processing, energy and tourism.

India-Tajikistan Relations

India and Tajikistan has greater significance for bilateral relations taking into consideration the geographical distance between two nations, which is less as compared to other Central Asian states. Both nations exchanged number of regular high level visits like Tajik President Emomali Rakhmonov visited India in 1995, 1999, 2001 and 2006 and Prime Minister of India Mr. Vajpayee visited Tajikistan in 2003 and 2006 and President of India Pratiba Devsingh Patil also visited this country in 2009. In these visits several agreements were signed such as Economic and Trade Cooperation; Technical Cooperation; Cooperation between Commercial Banks for Economic Activity of Tajikistan and State Bank of India, Indo-Tajik Joint Commission for Economic, Scientific and Technological Cooperation and the Bilateral Investment Protection Agreement for strengthen and deepen bilateral relations[64].

Consequently, the overall total trade between India and Tajikistan have increased from US$ 4.09 million in 2002-03 to US$ 12.13 million in 2005-06 to US$ 41 million in 2010-11 but it fell to US$ 28.37 million in 2011-12.

---

[63] I. Mavlonov. (2006). Central Asia and South Asia: Potential of India's Multilateral Economic Diplomacy in Inter-Regional Cooperation. *Strategic Analysis*, 30 (2): 431.

[64] A. Sarma. (2010). *India and Central Asia: Redefining Energy and Trade Links.* New Delhi: Pentagon Press, p.57.

Particularly India's exports to Tajikistan increased from US$ 3.55 in 2000-01 million to US$ 6.6 million in 2004-05 to US$ 21.28 million in 2011-12. However, India's imports from Tajikistan were fluctuating trend (Figure 4.3). India experienced surplus trade balance upto 2007 and thereafter trade balance was in the favour of Tajikistan.

Fig. 4.3: **India's Trade with Tajikistan ($US Million)**

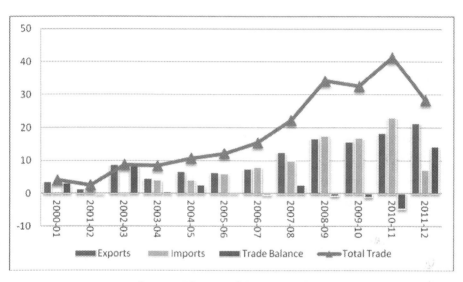

Source: *Ministry of Commerce, GOI.*

The major items of export from India to Tajikistan include pharmaceuticals products (HS 30: $US 8.14 million), meat & preparation (HS 02: $US 4.67 million) and readymade cotton (HS 61: $US 3.54 million) in 2011-12. While as nuclear reactors (HS 84), surgical products (HS 90) and glass & glassware (HS 70) were also exported to Tajikistan. The major import items were aluminium (HS 76: $US 5.64 million), vegetable soaps etc (HS 13: $US 1.15 million) in 2011-12.

India-Turkmenistan Relations

The bilateral relation between India and Turkmenistan began to build up from December 26, 1991 with high-level exchange of visits; as a result India established its embassy in Turkmenistan in January 30, 1994.[65] The political relations starts to flourish, when the president of Turkmenistan, Saparmurat Niyazov visited India in 1992 and 1997 and Prime Minister of India, P. V. Narasimha Rao visited Turkmenistan in 1995. In addition with several other ministerial visits, in which number of agreements were signed such as Investment Promotion and Protection agreement in September 20, 1995, agreement on avoidance of double taxation (Appendix 4)

The total trade between India and Turkmenistan increased from 2000-01 to 2008-09 while as after 2008-09 the trend of total trade decreased (Fig. 4.4). The total trade increased from US$ 4.66 million in 2000-01 to US$ 30.08 million in 2003-04 and further to US$ 51.4 million in 2008-09. However, total trade decreased to US$ 43.95 million in 2011-12. The overall trade balance has been in favour of India as its exports improved from US$ 2.71 million in 2000-01 to US$ 36.09 million in 2007-08 to US$ 43.95 million in 2011-12. The growth rates of India's imports from Turkmenistan were also increasing but less than India's exports to Turkmenistan. The India's imports from Turkmenistan increased from US$ 1.12 million in 2000-01 to US$ 12.36 million in 2005-06 to US$ 19.46 million in 2011-12 (Table 4.4).

---

[65]   I. Mavlonov. (2006). *Op cit.,* 434.

Fig. 4.4:   India's Trade with Turkmenistan

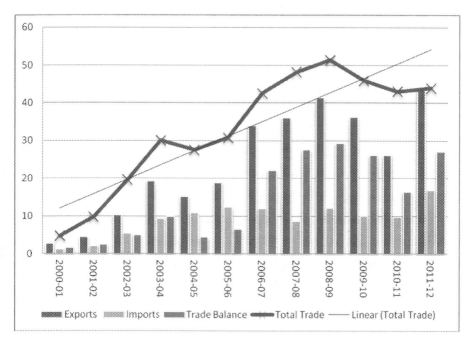

Source: *Ministry of Commerce, GOI.*

By and large export items from India to Turkmenistan include nuclear reactors and boilers (HS 84: US$ 13.08 million), pharmaceuticals products (HS 30: US$ 11.35 million), electrical machinery & equipments (HS 85: US$ 4.10 million), readymade garments (HS 62: US$ 3.45 million) and meat & preparation (HS 02: US$ 2.74 million) during 2011-12. India imports mainly comprise chemicals (HS 28: US$ 11.11 million) and cotton (HS 52: US$ 4.59 million).

India-Uzbekistan Relations

The cordial relationship between India and Uzbekistan are based on historical and cultural ties. After 1991, several high level visits have taken place between the two nations. Uzbek President Islam Karimov visited India in 1991 and 1994, signed an agreements on economic, scientific, and technical cooperation etc. In 1993, Prime Minister of India Mr. P. V. Narasimha Rao visited Uzbekistan, signed Indo-Uzbek Treaty on the Principles of Inter-State

Relations and Cooperation. In addition, of these visits, several other high-level views were exchanged and many agreements were signed (Appendix 5). In 1993, India and Uzbekistan Trade and Economic Cooperation Agreement was signed which includes Most Favoured Nation (MFN) treatment, industrial, scientific and technical cooperation, promotion of economic activities including active participation of small and medium sized enterprises to enhance bilateral economic cooperation. They also signed an agreement on avoidance of double taxation and bilateral investment promotion in 1999.

The total trade between India and Uzbekistan showed an upward trend (Fig. 4.5). The total trade increased from US$ 19.97 million in 2000-01 to US$ 52.57 million in 2004-05 to US$ 116.57 million in 2008-09. In 2011-12, it increased to US$ 150.97 million. Among Central Asian States, only Uzbekistan has experienced a favourable trade balance. While as in other CARs trade balance has mostly remained in favour of India. India's exports to Uzbekistan has significantly increased from 2003-04 which accounted US$ 15.14 million to US$ 29.69 million in 2006-07 to US$ 89.39 million in 2011-12.

Fig. 4.5: India's Trade with Uzbekistan

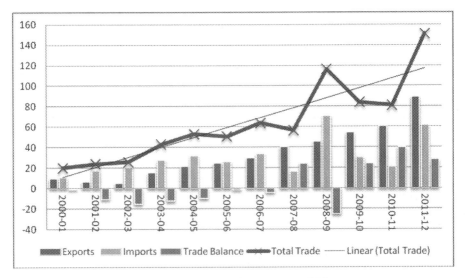

Source: Ministry of Commerce, GOI.

The exports items of India to Uzbekistan mainly comprise drugs and pharmaceuticals (HS 30), vehicles (HS 87), surgical products (HS 90) and nuclear reactors & boilers (HS 84) in 2011-12. India's imports from Uzbekistan improved since 2000-01, from US$ 10.58 million to US$ 31.46 million in 2004-05 to US$ 61.58 million in 2011-12. Currently, the main export items of India to Uzbekistan are pharmaceutical products (44 percent), vehicles (14 percent) and surgical products (8 percent). India's major import items are non-ferrous metals with share 48 percent and fertilizers 26 percent.

India-Central Asia Trade: Some vital Ratio and Indices

The various aspects of India-Central Asia mutual trade have been examined by using the various ratios and indices. These ratios and indices include Export-Import Ratio, Revealed Comparative Advantage and Gravity Model. They show the potential and advantage of India-Central Asian States economic relationship.

Export-Import Ratio: The imports of country must be managed in such a way that the overall import spending is within the safe limits set by the export earnings in order to avoid undesirable external borrowings (Brar, 1996). However, in case of India and Central Asian States, mismatch of exports and imports have always remained characteristic feature of their trade relations. The Triennium Averages (TAs) of ratios of India's exports to her imports for CAR's and the world is given in table 4.6.

Table 4.6: Ratios of India's Exports to her Imports: Central Asian States v/s Overall (Triennium Averages)

Triennium Average	Kazakhstan	Kyrgyzstan	Uzbekistan	Tajikistan	Turkmenistan	Overall
1997-2000	129	1724	232	1813	82	57
2000-2003	417	791	43	204	684	86
2003-2006	487	4388	710	163	124	73
2006-2009	103	3389	95	341	103	64
2009-2012	120	3157	174	290	119	64
Average Ratio (1997 to 2012)	251	2689	250	562	222	68

Note: The values are in percentages.
Source: *Ministry of Commerce, GOI.*

The export-import ratio fluctuates continuously with all. In case of Kazakhstan, the export-import ratio has increased from 129 percent during TA (1997-2000) to 487 percent during TA (2003-2006). However, TA in (2006-2009) was declined by 103 percent. Then again, it has increased to 120 percent in TA (2009-2012). There are many interpretations offered by several scholars regarding this fluctuation, however, major interpretation is that the export-import ratio of India and Kazakhstan fluctuates as India was increasing its imports from Kazakhstan.

The analysis of export-import ratios of India with other Central Asian States (Table 4.6) indicates that India exports more than their import that is why export- import ratio is sometimes around four digits and sometimes three. Overall, India's export-import ratio with CARs was 57 percent in TA (1997-2000) and it increased to 86 percent in TA (2000-2003). Afterwards, that it declined to 64 percent in TA (2009-2012). During the period 1997 to 2012, on an average, India was in position to meet her 68 percent bill of overall imports through the earning from overall exports, while as in case of Central Asian States its exports were able to pay the bill of imports.

Revealed Comparative Advantage (RCA)

Revealed comparative advantage has been applied in this section to analyze the comparative advantage between India and CARs. The results obtained reveals that India has RCA >1 in several items, which means that India has comparative advantage in exporting these products to CAR's. These potential items include chemicals and pharmaceuticals, machinery and transport equipment, iron and steel articles, ores and minerals and petroleum products.

Chemicals and Pharmaceuticals (HS-30): These items have export potential to Central Asian States and are among major export items from India to this region. During 2009-12, India exported US$ 308.01 million of chemicals and pharmaceuticals products to CARs, accounting 31.01 percent of India's total exports. There are other export potential items related with HS 30 such as carbonates (HS-2836), animal and human blood for therapeutic uses (HS-3002), medicaments (HS-3004) and fungicides, herbicides and insecticides (HS-3808).

Coffee and Tea (HS-09): This item has also export potential to CARs, but it is marginally exported. During 2000-03, India exported US$ 62.38 million, accounting 26.25 percent and during 2009-12, its export share declines to 13.7 percent. Some other items including in this category are cream and milk concentrated (HS-0402), vegetable saps (HS-1302), animal or vegetables oils (HS-1516), sugar confectionary (HS-1704).

Cotton (HS-61): Among CARs, India exported this item only to Kazakhstan, Kyrgyzstan and Tajikistan. The export potential of this commodity increased from US$ 14.01 million, accounting 5.9 percent in 2000-03 to US$73.86 million in 2003-06, accounting 15 percent. However, its percentage share declined to 6.54 percent in 2006-09 and 5.9 percent in 2009-12

Machinery and Transport equipment: In these commodities also India has comparative advantage to export, these items form the major share in CAR's import basket. These countries mainly import these commodities from Russia, China, Germany, US and Ukraine. Other items including in this category are refrigerators and freezers (HS-8418), air vacuum pumps (HS-8414), pumps for liquids (HS-8413), laboratory equipments (HS-8419), machines and mechanical appliances (HS-8473), transistors (HS-8524), wires and cables (HS-8544), public transport motor vehicles (HS-8702), motor cars (HS-8703), spare parts and other accessories (HS-8708).

There are other export potential items like lead ores and concentrates, petroleum products, cosmetics, soaps and organic products, plastic articles, rubber articles and medical and surgical products in which India could enjoy comparative advantage in exporting to CAR's.

Similarly, Central Asia States has RCA >1 in many potential export items to India. The present level of trade is less than its actual potential. In 1996, India imports few items from CAR's but onwards number of import items increased. The export potential items includes: natural and cultured pearls or semi precious stones (HS-71), zinc and articles thereof (HS-79), salt, sulphur, earth and stone, plastering materials, lime, and cement (HS-25), inorganic chemicals, organic and inorganic compounds of precious metals (HS-28), lead and articles thereof (HS-78), nuclear reactors, boilers, machinery mechanical appliances parts thereof (HS-84) and iron and steel (HS-72), flat-rolled products of iron (HS- 7208), ferrous-alloys (HS-7202), iron and steel rods (HS-7214), tubes (HS-7304), and pipes (HS-7305).

Gravity Model

To study the actual and potential trade between India and CAR's, Gravity Model is employed here. The dependent or responsive variable in this model is total trade between participating countries; while the independent variables in this model are GDP at current price, distance, and per-capita income. The purpose of this model is to exactly determine the impact of given variable on trade between given countries. Gravity Model equation has been employed for the time period t = 2000-2012 and for a cross-section of 6 countries, including India (jth country) which implies 5 pairs of cross section observations:

Table 4.7 depicts the estimated results Gravity Model, which indicates that both product of GNI and distance have significant value. The bilateral trade between India and Central Asian States will increase by 0.68 percent as the product of GNI increases by 1 percent. Similarly, the coefficient of distance shows that when the distance between India and CAR's increases by 1 percent, bilateral trade decreases by 0.87 percent. Therefore, both coefficients are empirically reliable with gravity model assumptions, i.e., India's trade is directly proportional to the economic size of the trading partners and inversely proportional to the distance between them.

Table 4.7: Estimated Results of two Gravity Models for India

Explanatory Variables	Model 1		Model 2	
	OLS Coef.	Std. Coef.	OLS Coef	Std. Coef
Constant	2.50		1.002	
GNI	0.685	0.45	0.463	0.096
PCGNI			0.39	0.149
Distance	-0.864	0.50	-1.81	0.601
R^2	0.789		0.810	
Ad. R^2	0.782		0.800	

Source: *The values of these variables are derived through SPSS 16.*

The augmented gravity model for India and CAR's has been estimated, which included PCGNI variable to analyse its impact on bilateral trade as shown in model 2. The coefficients of model 2 are shown also in table 4.7. The data in the table portrays that GNI is statistically significant. India's trade with CAR's increases by 0.46 percent as the product of GNI increases by 1 percent. Likely, 1 percent increases in distance, decreases 0.80 percent of bilateral trade of India with CAR's. However, PCGNI is other explanatory variable included in the augmented gravity equation. Its coefficient is 0.39, which determine that trade increases between trade participating countries, but less than proportionally.

Trade Potential of India with CAR's

The trade potential of India with CAR's could be predicted through the Gravity Model equations of bilateral trade flows. The estimated coefficients were used to predict the trade between trading countries based on given data of GNI, PCGNI and distance. Then predicted value trade is compared with actual trade. We have estimated the model 2 for India and CAR's for a period of 2000-2012. The ratio (P/A) is predicted value (P) and actual value (A) of India with CAR's to assess the trade potential and also used to forecast the direction of future trade. If the ratio of (P/A) is greater than unity, it indicates that India has potential to expand trade with respective country and vice versa. We divide data into five sub periods to estimate the ratio of predicted and actual trade value.

Table 4.8: India's Potentiality of Trade with CARs

Indicator Country	P/A 2000-2002	P/A 2003-2005	P/A 2006-2008	P/A 2009-2011	P/A 2012-13
Kazakhstan	1.10	2.06	4.17	7.9	10
Kyrgyzstan	0.55	0.64	2.93	8.5	10
Tajikistan	1.9	4.22	4.5	9	10
Turkmenistan	1.78	1.63	3.77	12	10
Uzbekistan	1.64	1.4	3.08	13	9

Note: Calculations are based on gravity model equations.

According the P/A ratio, India has adequate potential to enhance its trade with CAR's. The results show that India's actual bilateral trade with CAR's is below than its potential and similarly its trade relation with these countries is low compared to China, Russia and Iran etc. Table 4.8 shows that in 2000-2002 ratio (P/A) was greater than 1 for all CAR's except Kyrgyzstan but after 2006 onwards its ratio also increases significantly.

According to gravity model results, India has high trade potential with CAR's, while as the large difference in actual and estimated trade indicates that they are not utilizing their trade potentials. In order to decrease the difference between actual and estimated trade, trade promotional policies like increase in GNI and reduction in transport costs need to be adopted.

India's current trade with CAR's is low, as based on traditional commodities, and is difficult to improve in coming years. However, their relation with India cannot be viewed in the context of present trade situation. By 2015, India's trade with European, the CIS as well as Iran, Afghanistan and Pakistan could be range of US$500-600bn annually. Even if road networks conducted 20 percent of this trade, US$100-120bn of Indian trade would pass through the GCA region.[66] It is expected that India will enhance its existing relation with this region in terms of oil, gas, textiles and nuclear trade, and these are key areas which could enhance trade between two regions and thereby make their relations strong and durable.

---

[66]   G. Sachdeva. (2011). 'India-Central Asian Economic Relations'. *In:* Laruelle M. and Perrouse S. (eds.) *Mapping Central Asia: Indian Perception and Strategies.* USA: Ashgate, p. 140.

CHAPTER 5

Economic Relation Between India-Central Asia

Along the increase in India's exports to the CAR's region, the commercial relations between the two regions is on progress. Central Asia is emerging as potential destination for India's overseas investment. Number of Indian companies has set up wholly owned and joint ventures in the CAR's in different sectors like: oil & gas, pharmaceutical, information technology, food products and petroleum products. The CAR's provide opportunities for Indian companies, such as London-based Indian steel tycoon Laxmi Mittal owns 5.5 million ton capacity steel plant, employing 50,000 people in Kazakhstan.[67] India has created an institutional framework to facilitate trade and investment and set up Inter-Governmental Commissions for economic, trade, technical and scientific cooperation with this region. Such relations are further institutionalised to set-up joint working groups in several fields as follows: Hydrocarbon, IT, military-technical, science and technology cooperation etc. Additionally, India extended credit lines and EXIM Bank in the CAR's increases Indian export without risk. This scheme provides contract value that is to be paid in advance by the importers and should be about 15 to 20 percent. Nevertheless, EXIM

---

[67]   G. Sachdeva. (2010). 'Regional Economic Linkages'. *In:* N. Joshi (eds.), *Reconnecting India and Central Asia: Emerging Security and Economic Dimensions.* Washington DC and Sweden: Central Asia-Caucasus Institute Silk Road Studies Programme, p. 140

Bank disburses the remaining contract upon the delivery of goods and also takes care of the recovery of credit provided to foreign buyers, without taking help of Indian exporter. Besides, Double Taxation Avoidance Agreement has also been signed to promote and facilitate trade.

To give fillip to their economic relations, India has developed banking relations with the CAR's. Canara Bank of India has developed connection with Commercial Bank for Foreign Economic Affairs of Tajikistan, National Bank for Foreign Economic Activity of Uzbekistan and State Bank for Foreign Economic Affairs of Turkmenistan[68]. India and CAR's signed various agreements for economic cooperation under International Technical and Economic Cooperation. In addition, Federation of Indian Chambers of Commerce and Industry creates Joint Business Councils with Kazakhstan, Uzbekistan and the Kyrgyzstan.[69] Kazakhstan provides opportunity to Indian industries to invest in extraction of sunflower oil, wool, wheat production, leather, construction of houses and hotels.[70] Other areas that have been identified for cooperation include energy, textiles, information technology, food processing, education and petrochemicals[71].

There are large prospects that trade and investment between India and Central Asia would enhance fast in future, and long-term relations have been in the process of development, which will increase the trade between the two regions. The CAR's are mainly dependent on external sector, which could be an opportunity for India to invest in potential export sectors such as textiles, chemicals, aluminium, oil and gas and agriculture products. Besides, India expects to achieve access to CAR's through technology and can enhance its trade and commercial relations through export of IT items and can provide health, education and other services through the export of information

---

[68]   Ibid., p. 141

[69]   Ibid., P. 142

[70]   *http; www.ficci.com.* (Accessed on 11-10-2012).

[71]   R. Agarwal. (2006). Towards Comprehensive Economic Co-operation between India and Central Asia Republics, New Delhi: Research and Information System for Developing Countries, p. 6.

technology. In IT sector India has comparative advantage to export and CAR's are in need and have advantage to import these items from India.[72]

Altogether, The CAR's has much potential, but India has least presence in this region. The Indian Commerce and Industry Minister launched CIS programme in 2003. The objective of this programme was to enhance India's economic relations with the following seven countries in the first phase namely Azerbaijan, Kazakhstan, Kyrgyzstan, Tajikistan, Turkmenistan, Ukraine and Uzbekistan. In order to make this programme a success, exporters and business chambers were being supported for organizing trade fairs by government of India and CAR's trade delegations were also invited to visit India in order to promote market activities. As a result, the trading community of India had given a good response for enhancing the bilateral trade in future. The steps like economic liberalization, establishment of institutional mechanism of interaction and development of direct links had enhanced economic relations between CAR's and India. However, a lot needs to be done to realize the full potential. Keeping in view the need for increasing trade and the interest of businesspersons of both sides various meetings and other associated activities have been taken up at the top level.

India and Kazakhstan

India-Kazakhstan relations are cordial and progressing smoothly. After independence of Kazakhstan, India provided credit lines that facilitated Indian export goods, and developed commercial relations with rising private companies in Kazakhstan. As a result, in exporting medicines, number of India Pharmaceuticals companies made great efforts to establish joint ventures in Kazakhstan for manufacturing medicine. India exports mainly pharmaceutical items to Central Asia that fulfil 30 percent need of Central Asia.[73] There

---

[72] Bhaumik, (2004). 'Central Asian Economies: Prospects for India's Trade and Investment'. *In:* Indranil Banerjee (eds.), *India and Central Asia*. UK: Brunel Academic Publishers Ltd. p. 340.

[73] S. Peyrouse. (2010). 'Comparing the Economic Involvement of China and India in the Post-Soviet Central Asia'. *In:* Marlene L., Jean-Fancois H., Sebastien P. and Batram B. (eds.), *China and India in Central Asia: A New Great Game*. USA: Palgrave Macmillan, p. 168.

are number of joint ventures which have been created in this area, such as Gufic Avicenna, Reddy-Pharma and Shreya Life Scientist Pharmaceuticals. Kazakhstan represents a particularly interesting market in this domain, with an estimated worth of US$ 400 million per year and an availability of 6000 preparatory products of which only 10 percent are produced locally.[74]

These efforts have enabled India to get a strong foothold in growing market of Kazakhstan.[75] India is continuously inviting ministers, diplomats and opinion-makers from Central Asia to visit potential areas and creates relations with officials, politicians and businesspersons.[76]

In Kazakhstan, both wholly owned and joint ventures of India are mostly engaged in engineering procurement, construction, technical services, trading in tea, pharmaceuticals and insurance sectors. The Ispat-Karmat invested US$ 800 million in steel plant of Kazakhstan, produces annually 6 million tonnes of steel as a result Kazakhstan could enhance export of steel products and earn foreign exchange.[77] In 2004, Punj-Lloyd singed contract of US$ 35 million to produce pipes, this also helped the Kazakhstan for laying pipelines in Tengiz and Kondey.[78]

Kazakhstan launched non-industrial development and investment programme for the period of 2003 to 2015.[79] When President of Kazakhstan Nursulatan Nazarbaevs visited India in 2002, he declared that IT sector is main area for developing bilateral cooperation. Subsequently the first India-Kazakhstan Joint Working Group on IT sector was held in 2006 in Almaty.[80]

---

[74] Sathave (2008). India Kazakhstan Sign Five Pacts to Bolster Partnership, in Sarkaritel. Available on www.sarkaritel.com/news_features/january2009/27indkazakhstanpacts.htm (accessed on 12 May 2013)

[75] R. Gidadhubli. (2007). 'India-Kazakhstan Economic Relations'. *In:* K. Santhanam, Kuralay Baizakova and Ramakant Dwivedi (eds.), *India-Kazakhstan Perspective: Regional and International Interactions.* New Delhi: Anamaya Publishers, p. 34.

[76] M. Ibrokhim. (2006). Central Asia and South Asia: Potential of India's Multilateral Economic Diplomacy in Inter-Regional Cooperation, *Strategic Analysis.* 30(2): 429.

[77] R. Gidadhubli (2007). *Op cit.,* p. 34.

[78] Ibid., p. 34.

[79] S. Peyrouse (2010). *Op cit.,* p 169.

[80] Angira Sen Sarma (2010). *India and Central Asia: Redefining Energy and Trade Links.* New Delhi: Pentagon Press, p. 36.

The Chennai-based internet Business Factory India and State Education Centre Bilim set up technopole in Kazakhstan public school system and IBFI provide intranet system for national education system.[81] The India-Kazakhstan informational technology centre was opened first time at Al-Farabi University in 2005. The Indian IT companies, the National Association of Software and Service Companies (NASSCOM), participating in Indo-Kazakh IT sector cooperation and STPI Company of Bangalore open first IT Park in Kazakhstan.[82]

In April 2011, Prime Minister of India Dr. Manmohan Singh visited Kazakhstan and focused on enhancing economic relationships. Seven agreements were signed:

1. Kazmunaigas National Company and ONGC signed agreement on Satpayev exploration block
2. The India and Kazakhstan signed agreement for cooperation in judicious use of atomic energy
3. Joint Action Plan for Strategic Partnership between India and Kazakhstan (Road Map) for the period of 2011-114[83]
4. The Information Technology Department of India and Kazakhstan signed MoU for enhancing future cooperation
5. Agreement on Mutual Legal Assistance in civil matters
6. Both signed agreement related to agriculture and allied sectors for cooperation and
7. Signed an agreement on cooperation in the field of health sector.

---

[81] P. Sneha Chysolite (2001). IBFI and Republic of Kazakhstan Enter into Education JV in IT People. Available on www.itpeopleindia.com/20011203/careers1.shtml. (accessed on 23 June 2013).

[82] Indian Embassy in Kazakhstan (2006). India's Substantial Participation in IT park. Available on www.indianembassykaz.com (accessed on 22 December 2012).

[83] The Roadmap is the joint action plan for execution of projects to be taken up by both sides during 2011-14 for the implementation of Inter-Governmental Agreements. The roadmap highlights specific areas of bilateral cooperation in hydrocarbons, civilian nuclear energy, cyber security and space information technology, high-tech and innovative technology, healthcare, pharmaceuticals, agricultural and cultural exchanges.

Among CARs, Kazakhstan is hub of energy resources and India is making elaborate efforts to enhance its presence and participation in this sector. According to former Petroleum and Natural Gas Minister, Mini Shanker Aiyer, India is looking this sector keenly for creating joint ventures with Kazakhstan. The ONGC and GAIL of India are participating in Kazakhstan's energy sector.[84] In 2011, ONGC decided to purchase 25 percent stake in Kazakhstan's oil exploration block and enter into oil and gas sectors.[85] Thus, energy potential of Kazakhstan could play a vital role for India's energy needs. Kazakhstan transport oil from Caspian Sea to northern ports of Iran, while as Iran exports same amount of oil from its southern ports to world market. There is great opportunity for India to promote mutual economic ties with Kazakhstan.[86]

India-Uzbekistan

The economic relation between India and Uzbekistan increased after the agreement on approval of credit line signed by India for US$ 10 million in 2000. In 2005, President Islam Karimov visited India and signed twelve agreements/ MOUs for cooperation in military and technical areas, culture and sports, small and private entrepreneurship and education. The MoUs were also signed in IT, tourism, education and banking.[87] India and Uzbekistan have also growing economic relation with many potential areas. GAIL India, signed MoU for US$ 60 million in 2006 for natural gas and oil exploration. Many Indian companies have joint ventures in different areas such as in pharmaceuticals products, leather, and manufacturing of cotton. Similarly, many approved Indian companies have completely owned subsidiaries in following sectors such as leather products, readymade garments, hotels, restaurant, pharmaceuticals, and drugs.[88]

---

84   R. Gidadhubli (2007). *Op cit.,* p. 35.

85   The Hindu (20 April 2011). Toe-Hold in Kazakhstan.

86   Gidadhubli, (2007). *Op cit.,* 36.

87   M. Ibrokhim (2006). *Op cit.,* p. 436.

88   Export-Import Bank of India. (2007). CIS Region: A Study of India's Trade and Investment Potential. New Delhi: Quest Publications, Occasional Paper No. 116, p 102.

Uzbekistan has considerable interest in IT sector of India. In October 2004, India and Uzbekistan signed MoU for set up of India-Uzbek IT centre, with Rs 30 million assistance for this centre, which is known as Jawaharlal Nehru IT Centre in Uzbekistan. This centre was inaugurated in April 2006 by Prime Minister of India and was upgraded under the joint action plan in 2011, during the visit of Minister of State for Communication and IT Sachin Pilot to Tashkent. Further, MoU on IT sector cooperation was signed in May 2011, during President Karimov's visit to India. The STPI Bangalore participated actively in Uzbekistan and also formed IT Centres in Tashkent and Dushanbe. The memoranda of intent was signed in 2006 to establish IT Centres also in Ashgabat and Bishkek. India provides US$ 65 million grant to open Indo-Uzbek IT centre in Tashkent University.[89]

Moreover, the markets for Indian pharmaceutical companies are growing in Uzbekistan. For further progress, it requires facilitation like joint ventures and wholly owned subsidiaries. In the 9th session of inter Government Commission of Indo-Uzbek in 2006, main issue was related to pharma and health sector. After this session, the government of India took steps to enhance pharma export to Uzbekistan. The delegation of 22 pharmaceuticals companies visited Uzbekistan and interacted with the local companies. In Uzbekistan, several Indian pharma companies have joint ventures, such as Core Healthcare, Ajanta Pharma, Dr. Reddy's and Gufic of Mumbai.

Uzbekistan is the seventh largest cotton producer in the world with 4 percent share of total world production and is the second largest exporter of cotton in the world. Similarly, in this potential sector India develops cooperation with Uzbekistan. Uzbek Minister I. Khaydarov visited India and held that our nation is looking for collaboration of Indian textiles industry in our cotton sector and I am planning to interact with five or six Indian textile companies. He also stressed for joint ventures and to setup 100 percent, fully individually owned companies.' The Indian textile company Spentax acquired two textiles mills in Tashkent, invested US$ 81 million and known as Spentex Tashkent Toytepa.[90] The Indian textile company spentex has 100 percent own

[89]   S. Peyrouse. (2010). *Op cit.,* p. 168.
[90]   http://mea.gov.in/foreignrelation/uzbekistan.pdf (accessed on 22 April 2011)

production facility and is working in Uzbekistan from the last several years. Similarly, Texprocil and Uzbek Govt. signed a MoU in November 2006 for the production of cotton products. In 2007, 16 member trade delegation from Tamilnadu visited Uzbekistan to set up textile units.[91]

India and Uzbekistan has economic relation in other sector also such as small and medium scale business, tourism and railways. India invested in Uzbek railway infrastructure and aviation area, which is also viable area for India. Uzbekistan is fourth largest producer of gold in the world and India shows its interest in this area in April 2007, when Minister of state for Commerce Jairam Ramesh visited Uzbekistan. As a result, Uzbek government accepted proposal of Indian MMTC/National Mineral Development Corporation (NMDC) for gold exploration in addition with development of the gems and jewellery sector.[92] Larsen and Toubro Indian based construction company constructed 500 bed capacity international hotel at Samarkand and 440 bed hotel at Bukhara and coupled with advanced tobacco factory at Samarkand.[93]

India-Kyrgyzstan

From the beginning, India and Kyrgyzstan were interesting to develop deeper economic cooperation and in this regard Indo-Kyrgyz joint commission was set up in 1992 and its second and third meeting was held in Bishkek in 1997 and New Delhi in 2003 respectively. In 1999, an agreement on avoidance of double taxation was signed, that stimulated investment flows, technology, trade and services. Kyrgyzstan has given great significance to India for cooperating in various fields such as tourism, information technology, food processing, pharmaceuticals, engineering goods, banking services, education, setting up small and medium scale business units, and mining. The Indo-Kyrgyz Joint Commission for economic, science and technical cooperation and Joint

---

[91] M. Gunasekaran, "Exporters explore possibilities of setting up mills in Uzbekistan. The Hindu, June 15, 2007. Available on www.hindu.com /2007/06/15/stores. (accessed on 20 December 2012)

[92] http://www.commerce.nic.in/April07release.htm (accessed on 12 August 2012)

[93] Angira Sen Sarma (2010). *India and Central Asia: Redefining Energy and Trade Links.* New Delhi: Pentagon Press, p. 46.

Business council has been formed to strengthen and support bilateral trade and economic relations.[94]

In 1995, India offered a credit of US$ 5 million to Kyrgyzstan to promote new and medium scale units, modernize industrial units and to finance joint ventures.[95] Indian Prime Minister in 2003 granted US$ 2 million for the establishment of mini hydel station in Kyrgyzstan.[96] According to the protocol of the joint Commission of September 2007, the government of India waive off debt amounting US$ 1.024 million.[97] India assisted IT Development Centre and a potato plant in Kyrgyzstan and a MoU was signed in Bishkek on March 20, 2006. Moreover, Indian potato processing plant and techno-economic team imparting training to Kyrgyz people.

The India set up mountain medical research centre in Kyrgyz. DIPAS (Defense Institute of Physiology and Allied Sciences, New Delhi) acts as nodal agency in this venture. India also donated medical equipment to Kyrgyzstan that accounts Rs. 2.2 million in 2005.[98] The BIOCON Ltd. has entered into joint venture with Nobex Corp and starts its production of bio-drugs in February 2006. Another Indian company M/s Jagson Oil opens four petrol pumps, with an investment of about US$ 2 million.[99] The Channel Plastic Indian based company has completed plastic dishware plant in the Special Economic Zone of Bishkek, with the investment of US$ 1 million. There are other Indian companies entering into joint ventures in the coal, mineral and hotel construction in Kyrgyzstan. The Komur Mash Mining established by Indian and Kyrgyzstan entrepreneurs is another joint venture for molybdenum

---

[94] Available at www.eurasianet.org/resource/kyrgyzstan/hypermail/200311/0017.shtml.

[95] Ties with Central Asia, National Herald, 25 September, 1995.

[96] Embassy of India, Kyrgyzstan-basic facts. Available at http://meaindia.nic.in

[97] I. Musaeva. (2008). 'Prospects of Kyrgyz-India Economic Cooperation'. *In:* K Santhanam and Ramakant Dwivedi (eds.), *India-Kyrgyzstan relation Perspective and Prospects.* New Delhi: Anamaya Publishers, p.38.

[98] Embassy of India, Kyrgyzstan-basic facts, available at http://meaindia.nic.in (accessed on 23 May 2011)

[99] S. Pandey (2008). 'Indo-Kyrgyz Relations: The Search for New Horizons'. *In:* K Santhanam and Ramakant Dwivedi (eds.), *India-Kyrgyzstan relation Perspective and Prospects.* New Delhi: Anamaya Publishers, p. 8.

and their volume of investment in this project has been US$ 35 million. India is also imparting technical assistance to Kyrgyzstan under the Indian Technical and Economic Cooperation (ITEC) program, for human resource development. The Information Technology centre was created in 2007 in Bishkek for which India provided grant of Rs. 47.8 million grant. The centre has advanced technology for the development of software and personal training. This centre was inaugurated by Indian Oil and Gas Minister Mr. Murli Deora. It is also expected that IT sector cooperation will further increase.

India-Turkmenistan

After independence of Turkmenistan, India provided financial and technical assistance to this nation. Until recently, the Indian-Turkmenistan economic relation is however, underperform, with only one joint venture Turkmenistan-Ajanta Pharma Ltd. that provided loan accounting US$ 15 million in 1998. This joint venture does have latest technology and produces 70 types of medicines.[100] Turkmenistan seeks to promote investment relation with India through joint ventures in other areas like juice making, food and wool processing sectors. In 2009, chamber of Commerce and Industry of Turkmenistan and the India-CIS Chamber and Industry signed mutual agreement for enhancing economic and trade relation. As a result, trade between two countries increased to 20 percent in 2010 and 2011. Twelve Indian construction companies enter into Turkmenistan economy in 2010-11. The Indian trade bodies such as CII, FICCI, and ASSOCHAM have been busy to enhance trade and investment through sending regular business delegation to Turkmenistan.

The Turkmen-Indian Industrial Training Centre has been functioning in Ashgabat since December 2002. Machine tools worth over a million US$ have been gifted to the Centre by Indian Govt. under ITEC program. India provides educational facilities for young professional of Turkmenistan under ITEC and ICCR fellowship programmes. The India-Turkmenistan Centre for Information Technology (ITCIT) was set up in October 2011. India has

---

[100] Turkmenistan-Basic Facts, available at http://164.100.17.21/foreign_relation/turkmenistan.pdf, (accessed on 29 October 2007).

comparative advantage in IT sector, sends its experts to Turkmenistan for the development of information and communication technology, e-governance, telecommunication network.

India-Tajikistan

The relation between India and Tajikistan is growing due to some mutual, regional and international issues. In 1995, India provided extended credit line of US$ 5 million to Tajikistan for setting up joint venture with Ajanta Pharma. The same was converted into grants by Mr. Vajpayee the then Prime Minister of India in 2003 and gave second credit line US$ 25 million for increasing bilateral economic relations and defence cooperation in addition to combat terrorism. The second credit line was again offered during the visit of President Romanov's to India in August 2006 in addition a grant of US$ 8 million was also announced. Further India established IT centre in 2006 at Dushanbe, with grant of US$ 0.6 million with the help of Centre for Development of Advanced Computing (CDAC), providing equipment and training to the faculty members. However, Tajik National Centre will administer the IT centre for patents and information, which is regulated by Ministry of Economic and Foreign Trade.

Tajikistan has great horticulture potential such as growing cherries, apples, figs, melons, lemons, peaches, plums,[101] but Tajikistan is not able to reap the appropriate benefits of this potential due to lack of infrastructure such as basic inputs and cold storage. In this field India has used its experience and also gave a grant of US$ 0.6 million to set up fruit processing plant in Dushanbe. The HMT International Bangalore executed the project. On 26 January 2005, the plant was commissioned and began its production. In August 2006, President of Tajikistan Mr. Rahmon visited India and India agreed to help him in rehabilitating and modernizing of a Vintage Varzob-1 Hydro Power Station of 1936 with the help of Bharat Heavy Electricals Limited (BHEL) and National Hydroelectric Power Corporation (NHPC). The estimated cost of the project

---

[101] M. Kumar. (2007). 'India-Tajikistan Relations and the Quest for Regional Stability'. *In:* K. Santhanam and Ramakant Dwivedi (eds.), *India-Tajikistan Cooperation Perspective and Prospects.* New Delhi: Anamaya Publishers, p. 28.

was approximately US$ 20 million fully financed by India. With the result, the capacity of the project increased from 2x3.67 MW to 2x4.75 MW. Minister of Energy and Industry of Tajikistan and the India ambassador inaugurated the project on 28 December 2010.

Moreover, President Mr Rahmon paid official visit to India in the first week of September 2012, and discussed on establishing developmental projects such as IT Centre for excellence, electronic networking which includes tele-education and tele medicine, Entrepreneurship Development Institute and setting up small development projects. India also supported Tajikistan's accession to WTO as a result Mr.Sharif Rahimzoda, Minister of Economic Development and Trade and Ambassador Mr. Asith Bhattacharjee signed a Protocol supporting Tajikistan's accession to the WTO on 3 August 2012.

India looks at CAR's as its immediate neighbourhood and has geostrategic, and economic interest in this region. With result, good relations between India and CAR's are in mutual interest and benefits. Further there are many factors like energy project, transport and communication, information technology, energy security, textiles, and tourism in addition peace and stability in the CAR's and Afghanistan seems to be most crucial factor for India's security. All these factors lead to inter-regional Cooperation between India and Central Asian region. Moreover, the awareness about improving economic cooperation demands concrete policy implementations so that the relation will be strong and meaningful. It is not out of place to mention here the words of the Indian Prime Minister Dr. Manmohan Singh, "if our region wishes to be a part of the dynamic Asia, which is emerging in our neighbourhood, then we must act and act speedily and without any further loss of time".

CHAPTER 6

Importance of Central Asian Energy Resources for India

Energy at times is supposed to be basic precondition to economic development. Energy plays a vital role to sustain long-term economic growth that in turn satisfies basic human needs, such as food and shelter. It also improves the political and cultural dimensions of development through enabling the national governments to maintain educational, public health and other civic amenities. Further prosperity that economic development brings in accelerates the demand for more energy inputs.

CAR's is a region highly bestowed by the large wealth of hydrocarbon resources. Besides, the region holds precious and strategic metals like gold and uranium. Since the region lies in the vicinity of India and share long historical relations, the presence of precious resources particularly oil and gas has large implication for the country (India) whose energy needs are large and rising fast.

Energy and Economic Potential in India

The economic development of India is very much depending upon the availability of adequate energy as the growth of economy causes an increase in the demand for energy. In India, the domestic consumption of energy is more than production. This imbalance in demand and supply creates a problem for the growth of growing economy. It is well reflected by the fact that India is the world's 11th energy producer, i.e. with only 2.4 percent of domestic energy production while being the world's sixth largest energy consumer, (3.5 percent) in the global energy market seventy percent of the total energy demand in India is met by domestic production of coal and the remaining 30 percent is met by the use of petroleum of which 65 percent is imported. The import of petroleum is going to increase to 90 percent of its total consumption.[102] To bridge this gap, India has to import cost effective energy products. The total energy consumption of all the energy products as shown in fig. 6.1. It indicates that coal has highest consumption 42 percent followed oil by 24 percent.

Fig. 6 1:   Total Energy Consumption in India

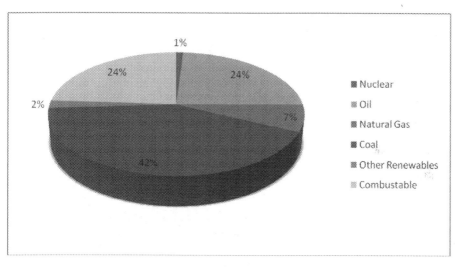

Source: *US Energy Information Administration*

Hydrocarbons constitute 42 percent of India's commercial energy consumption. According to the vision 2025 document, the share of oil and gas in the total energy supply will be 45 percent (oil 25 percent and gas 20 percent) by the 2025.[103] In the present scenario, India's energy consumption has changed from traditional or non commercial (fuel wood, dung and crop residues) to

---

[102]   South Asia Monitor, NO. 98 Sept. 7, 2006.
[103]   Energy Information Administration 2012.

commercial sources (coal, oil and gas)[104], but the domestic energy security is among the biggest challenge for Indian policy makers.

According to the new policy scenario of World Energy Outlook (WEO) 2011, India's demand will grow continuously, attain 1464 mtoe in 2035. The world's compound annual growth of energy is 1.3 percent from 2009 to 2035, but India's CAGR is estimated 3.1 percent for the same period, which is more than double of worlds energy demand. The share of India in the world's energy demand will increases to 8.6 percent in 2035 from 5.5 percent in 2009. Among all fuels, the demand of coal is higher will increases to 618 mtoe in 2035. Similarly, oil demand extensive growth increased to 356 mtoe in 2035 from 159 mtoe in 2009. The demand of other fuels also shows increasing growth (Fig. 6.2).

Fig. 6.2:   Total primary Energy Demand (TPED) in India, 2009-35 (Million Tones Oil Equivalent)

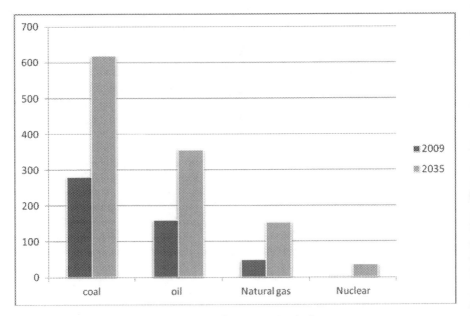

Source: *Energy Information Outlook, 2011*

---

[104]   Energy Information Administration 2012.

Figure 6.3 portrays the comparative status of production and consumption of oil in India. The gap between production and consumption of both oil increased, from 760.67 thousand barrels per day in 1998 to 942.75 thousand barrels per day, and consumption of oil increased from 18844.37 thousand barrels per day to 3292.21 thousand barrels per day in 2011. According to the Energy Information Administration and US Department of Energy, India's oil consumption growth rate is expected to increases from current 2.1 mb/d to 5.3 mb/d in 2025. Similarly, projection for imports will be 85 percent in 2025, mostly will be from import from Middle East, Central Asia and Africa.[105]

Fig. 6.3:   **Production and Consumption of Oil in India (Thousand Barrels Per Day)**

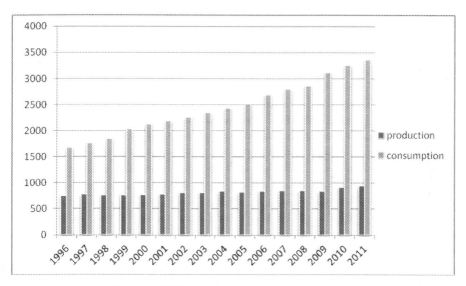

Source: *US Energy Information Administration*

The consumption of oil in India is increasing very high and there are apprehensions that by this trend domestic proven oil reserves will get exhausted by 2020. Due to this situation it is expected that India will be heavily depend on

---

[105]   S. Tonnesson and A. Kolas (2006). India's Energy Needs, in Energy Security in Asia: China, India, Oil and Peace, *Oslo (PRIO): International Peace Research Institute,* p.17.

imported oil.[106] India's dependence on imported oil has consistently increasing due to inactive domestic oil production and growing demand. This high dependency has negative consequence for financial health and energy security of the country. It indicates that India import dependence would continue to rise. The projected growth of demand is due to displeased demand for energy in India. The prime Minister and leading economist of India Dr Manmohan Singh has declared in an interview with Financial Times in 2004: "Energy security is second only in our scheme of things to food security".

In terms of gas, India holds 0.8 percent natural gas reserves of the world, while gas consumption is 1.9 percent of the worldwide; as a result, India import natural gas about 20 percent.[107] According the US Energy Information Administration, India's domestic supply and demand of gas was balanced before 2004; however, after 2005 the domestic production did not support the increasing demand for gas. In 2005, domestic production was 996 billion cubic feet and it increased to 1088 billion cubic feet in 2008 to 1682 billion cubic feet in 2011, but the consumption was more than production such as 1269 billion cubic feet in 2005, 1515 billion cubic feet in 2008 and 2261 billion cubic feet in 2011(Fig. 6.4). India's heavy and increasing dependence on imported gas, has compelled the country to import 92 billion cubic feet in 2004, 352 billion cubic feet in 2007 and 579 billion cubic feet in 2011.

---

[106]   Chudamani Ratnam (2005). The future of petroleum: An Indian perspective, paper presented at the 7th Asian Security Conference, New Delhi.

[107]   BP Statistical Review of World Energy 2011.

Fig. 6.4: India's Production and Consumption of Gas (Billion Cubic Feet)

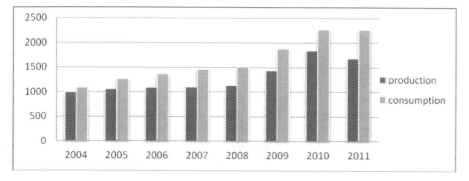

Source: *US Energy Information Administration*

Gas production and Liquefied Natural Gas (LNG) in India are located in western part of the country. Therefore, in western part of the country infrastructure of pipeline are available, but rest of the country is devoid of this facility. Thus, low accessibility of gas and inadequate infrastructure deteriorated gas market of India. It is expected that domestic supply of gas will increase by the KG-D6 block, coal bed methane in addition to new gas fields of ONGC and Gujarat State petroleum.

While India has world's fourth largest coal reserves, however, gap between demand and supply is continuously increasing. The domestic production of coal in India is lower than consumption. Hence, the country imports coal to maintain balance between domestic production and consumption. The share of coal in India is 31 percent in total energy consumption and about 70 percent of coal is used for generation of power.

Fig. 6.5: India's Production and Consumption of Coal (Thousand Short Tones)

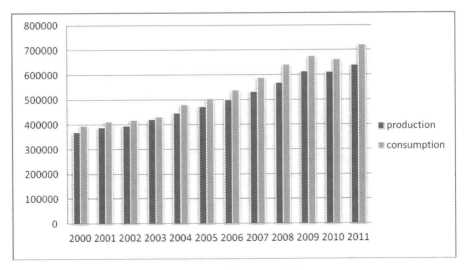

Source: *US Energy Information Administration*

(Fig. 6.5) portrays that in India, the gap between domestic production and consumption of coal is widening, and this could be attributed to industrial development that has gained all most a good momentum after 2000 onwards. Though the country has good quality and quantity of coal reserves, but due to the growing domestic demand, the available supply is falling short.

India is trying to explore more oil and gas within its own territory, which includes oil discovers in Rajasthan by U.K. based Cairn Energy and Gas discovers by India's Reliance industries of the coast of Andhra Pradesh in the Bay of Bengal. The country is also trying deepening its energy trade relationship with other countries, such as energy-rich region Persian Gulf and Central Asia. Currently, India is importing oil from Gulf Countries, Africa, and other middle East countries, and the major proportions of oil imports are from Africa which accounts 22 percent followed by Saudi Arabia 18 percent and Iran 11 percent and 34 percent from other middle east countries.

It shows that India is heavily dependent upon for energy products over the Middle East, North Africa and Iran supplies 67 percent of oil requirement as shown in above figure. The geopolitical volatility in Middle East, especially in

Libya and Egypt affects negatively on crude oil production in the region, as a result oil prices rise, which stimulates inflation in India.[108] According Goldman Sachs, increase in oil price by US$10 per barrel decrease GDP growth of India by 0.2 percent and increase inflation by 0.4 percent.

Given the major oil import sources of India, the on-going instability in the region and the US still not comfortable relations with Iran creates apprehensions in the minds of the country's (India's) policy planners to diversify its import sources of energy. Happily Central Asian republics offers an opportunity in this regard.

The energy rich Central Asian States have great significance for India. It is the area where India's foreign policy has the immediate connection with its economic growth plans. Therefore, India has opportunity to look towards CARs, which is best alternative for India. The collaboration between India and CARs in energy sector is one of the major areas of economic cooperation. Central Asian region is holding large energy resources. India has the potential and capacity to enhance its participation and presence in the various sectors in the said region.

Energy Reserves in Central Asia

The Central Asian region is called a "strategic region" because of the optimistic energy numbers.[109] The CAR's are considered the next oil and gas frontier, where proven oil reserves are between 15 billion to 31 billion barrels, which accounts for the 2.7 percent of world reserves. Similarly, proven natural gas reserves are at 230 to 360 trillion cubic feet comprising the 7 percent of the world reserves. Caspian region alone has huge expected energy potential, but still a considerable part of this potential is unexplored, as offshore oil and gas

---

[108] Economist Intelligence. (March 2011). *Oil and the Arab Worlds Unrest: Oil Pressure Rising.* Available on www.economist.com/blogs/newsbook/2011/02/arab_worlds_unrest_and_oil_prices (accessed on 29 July 2012)

[109] M. Crandall. (2006). 'Caspian Energy: Prospects, Pipelines and Problems'. In Energy, *Economics and the Politics in the Caspian Region: Dreams and Reality,* London: Praeger Security International, P. 10.

fields of Guneshli, Chiraq and Kyapaz in Azerbaijan are not fully utilized.[110] Nevertheless, on certain estimations the region potentially holds between 140 billion to 160 billion barrels of oil. There are five main basins of major oil and gas resources, including South Caspian, (extends to several regional countries), North Caspian, North Usturt and Mangyshlak, which are mainly in Kazakhstan and Amu-Darya in Uzbekistan. The statistical analysis of proven oil and natural gas reserves of CAR's are given in the following table.

Table 6.1: Proven Oil and Natural Gas (2013)

	Oil (Billion Barrels)		Natural Gas (Trillion Cubic Feet)	
	B P Statistical Review	Oil & Gas Journal	BP Statistical Review	Oil & Gas Journal
Country				
Kazakhstan	39000	30,000	85000	85000
Kyrgyzstan	NSR	0.40	NSR	0.200
Tajikistan	NSR	0.012	NSR	0.200
Turkmenistan	0.600	0.600	26000	26500
Uzbekistan	0.594	0.594	61000	65000

NSR: *Not separately Reported*
Source: *US Energy Information Administration.*

Kazakhstan is the largest of the former Soviet republic in the region. It possess enormous fossil fuel reserves and plentiful supplies of other mineral and metals such as iron ore, manganese, chromites, lead, zinc, copper, titanium, phosphate, sulphur, gold and silver. It has also a large agriculture sector. Kazakhstan's industrial sector rests on the extraction and processing of these natural resources and a growing machine-building sector specializing in construction equipment, agriculture machinery and some defence items. Similarly, Turkmenistan has significant hydrocarbon reserves in both oil and

---

[110] Amy Myers Jaffe (1998). Unlocking the Assets: Energy and the Future of Central Asia and Caucasus, *The James A. Baker Institute for Public Policy of Rice University*, p. 2.

natural gas, with some of the largest natural gas reserves in the world. On and offshore fields have been or are being developed, and the major fields include Barsa- Gelmes, Burun, Cheleken, Gograndag, Kamyshldzha, Korturtepe, Kum Dag, Kuydzhik, and the Okarem deposits.

Uzbekistan is a populous country in the region also possesses energy resources, particularly proven natural gas reserves. The country is the second largest producer of natural gas in Central Asia. However, the magnitude of proven oil reserves is believed to be much smaller than Kazakhstan. Significant increase in oil and natural gas production and lower energy demand in the past few years have allowed Uzbekistan to become nearly self-sufficient in energy. There are five oil and gas bearing regions in the country: Ust-Yurt, Bukhara-Khiva, Southwestern Gissar, Surkhandarya, and Ferghana. More than 150 oil and gas fields have been recently discovered, of which about 60 are currently in operation. The most important are Gazli, Shurtan, Kokdumalak and Mingbulak.

The Tajikistan is mountainous country with rich water reserves, therefore abundant potential in hydroelectricity. Its existing energy sector infrastructure is sparse and in need of rehabilitation. The Republic's greatest need in the energy sector is to facilitate strategic investment and cross-border trade. The favourable warm climate and long agricultural season as well as abundant river water resources for irrigation provide good conditions for specialization of the country in cotton production. Besides, there are minerals resources in the country in the form of certain amount of oil, mercury, coal, tin, zinc, marble, wolfram, and gold, silver, precious and semiprecious stones. The existing infrastructure is poor due to lack of investment and war condition that are main obstacles for growth of the economy.

Kyrgyzstan has potential for economic development, if the potential sectors receive greater attention, such as agriculture, agro-industrial sectors, minerals, service sectors and tourism. The country is depends about 60 percent of the energy products, though country has abundant hydroelectric resources. The harness of this vast hydroelectric energy resource would lay the basis for its future economic growth and development.

The Outlook of Primary Resources Energy

Oil: After the disintegration of USSR, the crude oil production decrease to 40 percent in the region. Nevertheless, it starts to regain after 1999 and oil was at its peak level in 2008. Kazakhstan's proven oil reserves were estimated at 30 billion barrels by the *Oil and Gas journal* 2012. As shown in table 6.2, production of oil is steadily increasing and the further proper utilization of its major oilfields could double its oil production by 2019 (EIA, 2012) and make Kazakhstan one of the world's top 5 oil producers within the next decade. That the country's main oil reserves are located in its western part such as Tengiz, Karachaganak, Aktob, Mangistau and Uzan. These onshore fields account for about half of current proven reserves, while the offshore Kashagan and Kurmangazy oil fields, in the Caspian Sea, are estimated to contain at least 14 billion barrels, with Kashagan accounting for around 9 billion barrels (EIA, 2012). Kazakhstan's current production is dominated by two giant fields: Tengiz and Karachaganak, which produce about half of Kazakhstan's total output. Kazakhstan's oil production reached 164 thousands billion barrels per day (bbl/d) in 2011; however, data for 2012 indicate that liquid production in Kazakhstan was slightly lower for the year at 1.60 million bbl/d. However, Kazakhstan's production has seen an impressive expansion since 1995 with the help from foreign oil companies. It surpassed the 1.0 million bbl/d production level in 2003 and steadily grew to be the second-largest oil producer in the Former Soviet Union, second only to Russia (EIA, 2012).

Karachaganak, also onshore north-western Kazakhstan close to the Russian border, produced 244,000 bbl/d of condensate between January and June 2012, accounting for about 15 percent of total production. According to Karachaganak Petroleum Operating (KPO), the field holds reserves of around 9 billion barrels of oil and gas condensate and 47 trillion cubic feet of natural gas. The KPO consortium under a PSA operates the field. KPO includes BG and Eni, (each 32.5 percent), Chevron (20 percent), and Lukoil (15 percent). Wood Mackenzie expects that production from Karachaganak is expected to increase to 340,000 bbl/d by 2020 (EIA 2012). On the other hand, Uzen oil field, located in south-western Kazakhstan in the Mangistau region, produced approximately 100,000 bbl/d in the first six months of 2012. It is 100 percent owned by KMG and has been in operation since 1961. The Uzen field is undergoing rehabilitation while the adjacent Karamandybas field is being developed as these two fields are expected to boost production. Similarly, Mangistau oil field, in the same region, produced 117,000 bbl/d between January and June 2012. It is operated jointly by KMG and China National Petroleum Corporation (CNPC).

Table 6.2: Total Oil Production and Consumption in CARs (Thousand Barrels Per Day)

Country		1991-1995	1996-2000	2001-2005	2006-2010	2011
Kazakhstan	Production	420.15	567.65	1089.7	1483.1	1640
	consumption	328.1	205.07	216.96	226.84	216.0
Kyrgyzstan	Production	1.98	1.85	1.64	1.153	0.95
	consumption	18.10	11.07	10.97	24.04	34.0
Tajikistan	Production	0.853	0.53	0.31	0.254	0.22
	consumption	15.02	19.10	27.83	21.20	14.0
Turkmenistan	Production	92.6	126.53	194.21	189.6	223.43
	consumption	67.16	60.60	85.91	93.88	110.0
Uzbekistan	Production	106.9	156.39	146.53	107.91	104.91
	Consumption	181.64	145.4	149.5	111.01	98.0

Source: *US, Energy Information Administration*

Turkmenistan had proven oil reserves of roughly 600 million barrels in January 2012 (EIA, Oil and Gas Journal). Oil production has increased in Turkmenistan from110,000 bbl/d in 1992 to 223,000 barrels per day in 2011. According to Turkmen official, the country aims to produce over 1.3 million bbl/d in offshore and onshore oil by 2030. The oil field are situated in the South Caspian Basin and the Garashyzlyk onshore area in the west of the country and section of the Caspian Sea contains 80.6 billion barrels of oil, though much is unexplored. The oil production in Turkmenistan has increased since 2007 and is highly dependent on new investment and technological capacity to tapped reserves.

The Oil and Gas Journal (OGJ) has assessed that Uzbekistan had 594 million barrels of proven oil reserves in 2012, 171 discovered oil and natural gas field, 51 of which produce oil and 17 of which produce gas condensates. The Ferghana Basin connects Uzbekistan, Kyrgyzstan and Tajikistan contains 4 billion barrels of oil including 3 billion of undiscovered reserves (US Geological Survey, USGS). According the table 6.2, oil production to some extent shows increasing trend, the average production of oil was 107 thousand billion barrels per day in 2006-2010 and for 2011 production of oil was 104.91 thousand billion barrel per day.

However, limited number of oil companies by now were present in Uzbekistan. But recently, several major foreign company entered the market for joint exploration projects with Uzbekneftegaz. Uzbekistan signed several production sharing agreements with foreign oil companies to develop existing fields and new basin in the region along the border with Turkmenistan. Lukoil and CNPC hold stakes in the Southwest Gissar and Bukhara-Kkiva oil basins respectively through agreements with Uzbekneftegaz.

Gas

Natural gas is spread in the whole Central Asian region, and is expected to have a great potential than oil. Characteristically Kazakhstan, Turkmenistan and Uzbekistan are considered among world leaders in natural gas production (Oil & Gas Journal, 2010). As for as Kazakhstan is concerned, it possess large quantities of natural gas and condensate. Energy experts estimate land –base reserves to be 18 billion cubic meters, with littoral reserves reaching up to 3.3 trillion cubic meters.[111] In January 2010, the Oil and Gas journal estimated Kazakhstan's proven natural gas reserves at 85 billion cubic feet (bcf). Natural gas production in Kazakhstan is almost entirely associated gas (EIA, 2010). It is expected that gas production will grow largely in the future. According to the Kazakh Ministry for Energy and Mineral Resources, Kazakhstan plans to increase its natural gas production to 1.84 bcf by 2015.

---

[111]   Ariel Cohen (2008). Kazakhstan: The Road to Independence Energy Policy and the Birth of a Nation, *Central Asia-Caucasus Institute and Silk Road Studies Program*, p. 163.

Table 6.3: Production and Consumption of Gas in CARs (Billion Cubic Feet)

Country		1991-1995	1996-2000	2001-2005	2006-2010	2011
Kazakhstan	Production	212.7	207.23	345.1	356.08	400.82
	Consumption	536.41	489.75	462.36	376.7	436.14
Kyrgyzstan	Production	1.85	0.56	0.79	0.72	0.35
	Consumption	64.63	66.96	39.64	24.10	14.12
Tajikistan	Production	1.52	1.61	1.34	1.16	0.67
	Consumption	50.9	41.73	47.03	19.9	7.03
Turkmenistan	Production	1676.6	1020.6	1994.4	2020.23	2337.8
	Consumption	150.9	189.29	502.7	699.45	209.8
Uzbekistan	Production	1615.7	1864.6	2103.6	2239.31	2226.3
	Consumption	1303.4	1446.50	1676.6	171.13	1802.5

Source: *Energy Information Administration, 2012*

The Karachaganak oil and gas field produced around 558 bcf gross gas in 2008, nearly half of Kazakhstan's total gross gas production. The expected gross gas production of Karachaganak was expected reach to 900 bcf by 2012 (EIA). The Tengiz oil and gas field produced 494 bcf gross gas in 2008 and production is expected to increase to 780 bcf by 2015. Another natural gas field, Amangeldy, is situated in the South of the country. The field was developed by Kazmunaigas, and the company expects production will increase. The Amangeldy fields that have been developed are producing approx. 10.6 bcf per year.[112] The development of Amangeldy field is important for Kazakhstan's energy security, as gas output from the field is geared to make the country self-sufficient in gas.

Turkmenistan currently ranks in the top sixth countries for natural gas reserves and top 20 in terms of gas production (EIA 2012). Turkmenistan is the second largest producer of natural gas (after Russia) in the former Soviet Union, and Russia is Turkmenistan's main recipient of natural gas exports. Turkmenistan's proven natural gas reserves increased from 94 tcf in 2009 to 265 Trillion cubic feet in 2012 (OGJ). There are world's largest gas fields,

---

[112] M. Crandall (2006). *Op cit.*, 25.

including with over 3.5 tcf of reserves located primarily in the Amu Darya basin in the Southeast, the Murgab Basin, and the South Caspian basin in the west. The Dauletabad field, located in the Amu Darya basin in the southeast is one of the largest gas-producing fields with estimated reserves of 60 tcf. In the year 2011, it was estimated that in the newly discovered south Yolotan depos field has potential reserves 460 tcf and possibly as high as 740 tcf, which would made south Yolotan the second largest field in the world (EIA 2012).

In Turkmenistan, natural gas has been mostly used for energy consumption. The country's consumption of total primary energy reached one quadrillion btu in 2009. Of this amount, approximately 78 percent was from natural gas, while 22 percent of the market share was from petroleum products (EIA 2012). The gross natural gas production showed increasing trend, 1615.7 bcf in 1991-1995 to 2226.3 bcf in 2011. However, the most complex issues related to oil and gas development in Turkmenistan transportation of hydrocarbons from Turkmenistan outside consumer markets. Current export routes are dominated by Russia that appears to be solidifying relationships with the Russian government to continue exporting the majority of natural gas through these existing pipelines. The Turkmen government has been trying to open more export routes in addition with existed pipelines. Turkmenistan has made many proposals with other countries to build infrastructure for exporting hydrocarbon. The pipelines with Iran and China and other routes are under consideration, Turkmenistan has export capacity nearly 3500 bcf/y (EIA 2012).

Uzbekistan has several hydrocarbon basins and is primarily a natural gas region. The most productive basins historically were in the gas-prone Amudarya region across the borders from Turkmenistan and in the oil fields of the Ferghana Vally.[113] These oil fields are dating from Soviet era and need investment to boost production. Uzbekistan holds an estimated 65 tcf of proven natural gas reserves as of 2012 (OGJ), ranking it the fourth highest in the Eurasian region and nineteenth in world (EIA, 2012). This country produces natural gas from 52 fields with 12 major deposits, accounting for over 95 percent of the country's gas production. Since 1992, Uzbekistan increased its natural gas production by 44 percent, from 1.5 tcf/y to over 2.1 tcf/y in

---

[113]   *Ibid.,* p 149.

2010. Recently Uzbekistan has been the second largest gas producer in the Eurasian region and ranks in the top thirteen natural gas producing countries in the world. Uzbekistan announced plans to spend $1 billion by 2020 on increasing gas reserves and infrastructure of fields in the south-western Gazli region.

In Tajikistan, only three companies are active in gas sector in addition to a state owned company. In the country, consumption is greater than production, therefore Tajikistan depends in gas imports from Uzbekistan and Turkmenistan. According to the Energy and Industry Ministry, the Tajikistan is building two oil refineries and is considering a third Avesta. The refineries under construction in Shakhrinav and Kanibad districts would be able to refine up to 100,000 tonnes of oil annually. President Emomali Rahmon has initiated the construction of country's first oil refinery. The annual production capacity of this oil refinery has been 100,00 tonnes of oil. It is expected that refinery capacity will increase to 500,000 tonnes per annum. (Business Monitor Online, July 2011).

Coal

Coal is another important abundant energy resource available in Central Asia, contributing nearly 23 percent of supply and 31 percent for heating purpose in 2005. The region has nearly 30 percent world's coal reserves. Among the newly independent states, Kazakhstan has abundant coal reserves. However, the production of coal declined by one third, mainly due to low economic efficiency. After independence, Kazakhstan introduced market mechanism in this sector also.[114]

---

[114] M. Crandall (2006). *Op cit.,* p 186

Table 6.4: Total Production and Consumption of Coal in CARs (Thousand Short Tonnes)

Country		1991-1995	1996-2000	2001-2005	2006-2010	2011
Kazakhstan	Production	117819.2	79077.17	90916.9	114055	128606
	Consumption	87903	54703.7	61353.9	82355.2	92076
Kyrgyzstan	Production	1427.5	485.9	471.35	527.35	931.45
	Consumption	2178.9	1291.9	1383	1201.74	1553.2
Tajikistan	Production	145.50	21.4	65.92	195.6	220.5
	Consumption	194.6	32.19	74.74	208.12	225.97
Uzbekistan	Production	4249.41	3140.7	2914.7	3739.3	3132.8
	Consumption	4980.8	3404.8	3588.5	3887.2	3227.6

Source: *US, Energy Information Administration*

Kazakhstan is one of the top ten coal producers in the world. The Pavlodar and Karaganda regions are important fields for coal production Kazakhstan, which accounts for 87.7 percent of the coal mined in the country. Kazakhstan has the eight largest reserves in the world, possessing four percent of the world's coal wealth. Kazakhstan produced 117819 tst in 1991-1995 and increased to 128606 tst in 2011, while consumed 87903 tst in 1991-1995 and 92076 in 2011 (table 6.4). The Kazakhstan shutdown unprofitable enterprises and all the coal companies are under private ownership. Due to private ownership resources are allocated efficiently, improving the exploitation of principle reserves, reducing cost of production and as a result, reducing the net cost of coal mining. In Uzbekistan coal reserves are located in Angren of Tashkent. In 1991-1995 coal, production was 4249.41 tst, but after that, its production decreased to 2914.7 in 2001-2005, but it increased to 3132.4 in 2011. As for as consumption is concerned it is more than production (Table 6.4). Similarly, in Tajikistan and Kyrgyzstan coal consumption is greater than production. These countries import coal from Kazakhstan and Russia.

Hydroelectricity

Tajikistan possesses vast and unique reserves of hydro-power resources. It occupies the 8th place in the world on absolute indicators of hydro resources. It owns about 4 percent of cost-effective hydro-potential of the earth and the 1st place on per capita hydro resources. Potential hydro power capacity of the country is 527 billion kWh. However, the industrial (technical) hydropotential is only 317.82 billion kWh, or 61.3 percent per year. Tajikistan is a mountainous country; it has 72 peaks with average elevation over 6,000 meters. Tian Shan, Gissaro-Alay and Pamir mountain systems cover 93 percent of Tajikistan's surface area. High mountains are always covered with snow and ice. Glaciers cover 6 percent of the total country's area and contain 550 cubic meters of water reserves. The Republic of Tajikistan is heavily dependent on hydroelectric power, with about 98 percent of the electricity generated in Tajikistan coming from hydroelectric sources and the balance of electricity is generated from fossil fuels.

Similarly, Hydropower is the only source of energy in Kyrgyzstan. The country has significant hydropower potential, which is however, not fully utilized. Hydropower accounts for around 90 percent of generated electricity and allows for exports to Kazakhstan, Uzbekistan, Russia and China. The electricity sector is largely unreformed, with a dominance of state ownership units and substantial tariff distortions.

Given the electricity potential of Central Asian republics, Tajikistan and Uzbekistan has vast hydro-electricity potential. Also other republics can also produce surplus electricity as these republics are rich in coal reserves in addition to oil an dgas. There is large electricity surplus forecasted for the region (Table 6.5).

Table 6.5: Surplus Electricity available for trade (GWH)

Country	Season	2005	2010	2015	2020	2025
Kazakhstan	Summer	3198	3623	6876	3745	-234
	winter	-2504	-2969	-130	-5563	-12318
	Annual	694	654	6746	-1818	-12552
Kyrgyzstan	Summer	4737	6283	6863	6406	5991
	Winter	-2092	1584	1517	5761	4753
	Annual	2645	7866	8381	12167	10744
Tajikistan	Summer	1511	4587	6767	12579	11697
	Winter	96	2841	4287	8308	7431
	Annual	1607	7429	11055	20887	19128
Uzbekistan	Summer	1620	3904	7635	5088	2091
	Winter	2862	5485	9846	7058	3767
	Annual	4482	9389	17481	12147	5858

Source: *World Bank*

From the whole discussion, it follows that Central Asian countries are rich in energy resources. While Kazakhstan, Turkmenistan and Uzbekistan are, rich in oil and gas while as Tajikistan and Kyrgyzstan have vast hydrogen-power potential. Hence, Central Asia offers an opportunity to India. India has large advantages in diversifying its energy sources and Central Asia as a source has multiple benefits.

CHAPTER 7

Opportunities and Challenges for India-Central Asian States Relations

The successful transition of Indian economy from inward to outward-oriented, stimulated a considerable economic growth. Though facing some major issues like energy security, infrastructure, regional disparities, poverty and internal security, India's external sector is growing and diversifying. Western countries were the main trading partners of India, but in recent year's diversification have taken place wherein, India is looking towards many regions and countries like Central Asia. Trade relations of India with the US and European Union have indeed increased in absolute terms, but in percentage share, it shows a decreasing trend. In this backdrop Indian economy is becoming highly integrated with Asia that has been reinforced by "India's Look East Policy."[115] India's integration within Asia is also evident from India-China trade as well as India's trade with Association of Southeast Asian Nations (ASEAN). These relations of India with Asian economies are even more deep than perceived,[116]

---

[115] G. Sachdeva (2010). 'Regional Economic linkages, in Nirmala Joshi'. In (ed.) *Reconnecting India and Central Asia: Emerging Security &Economic Dimensions*, Washington, DC: Central Asia Caucasus Institute (John Hopkins University), p. 114.

[116] J Ramesh (2008). India's Economic Integration with Asia. Paper presented at international conference on *Regional Economic Integration*, 24-26 November.

wherein, China, Japan and India are playing vital role in evolving Asian economic architecture.[117] It is however; felt that if India's economic relation within South Asia and with Central Asian region does not increase in tandem with the changing scenario, it will not have an effective hold.[118] For this purpose, India needs to develop economic policy framework that makes Pakistan, Afghanistan and CAR's to realize that the partnership will benefit them too. It will also help India to gain access to the energy resources in the Eurasian Region thereby.[119]

Undoubtly, the economic relations between India and CARs have vast potential for mutual benefits, which could be harnessed mainly through economic relations. Until recently, India and CAR's have signed number of agreements to promote and strengthen their relationships. There are many areas wherein the nature and scope of these relationships could be enlarged:

Opportunities

1. Central Asian States offer a relatively untapped market for Indian consumer goods. Consumers in this region have little choice, ranging from the highly priced, imported Western products to cheap but lower-quality Chinese manufactured goods, which have flooded the region. In this context, India's consumer goods including tea and pharmaceuticals have already acquired a foothold in this region. IT, banking, construction and food processing are also potential sectors for India to invest. There is also scope for India to assist Central Asian states in developing small and medium-scale enterprises. Moreover,

Proceedings available online at www.icainstitute.org. (accessed on 29 March 2012). See also M. Asher. (2007). *India's Rising Role in Asia*. Discussion Paper (RIS, New Delhi) No. 121.

[117] G. Sachdeva. (2011). 'Geoeconomics and Energy of India'. *In:* David Scott (eds.), *Handbook of India's International Relations*. London: Routledge, p. 48.

[118] *Ibid.*, p. 48.

[119] G. Sachdeva. (2010). 'Regional Economic linkages'. *In:* Nirmala Joshi (ed.) *Reconnecting India and Central Asia: Emerging Security and Economic Dimensions*, Washington, DC: Central Asia Caucasus Institute (John Hopkins University), p. 116.

Indian Government has assisted Indian entrepreneurs and business chambers to organise trade fairs under its CIS programme, and a joint business council has been setup in Kazakhstan. Currently, India is rather a piece-meal economic engagement in Central Asia.

2. Securing an assured and uninterrupted supply of energy is critical for keeping India's economic wheels in motion. Currently India imports 70 percent of its oil consumption from abroad; much of it's from the volatile Middle East region. Thus, energy security has become a central component of Indian national security and foreign policy. In this context, the rich energy resources of CARs have great significance for India, given its rising energy requirement and being an important strategic partner to CARs on equally advantageous basis. The hydrocarbon resources of this region are important for energy security of India. This region contains vast hydrocarbon fields both on-shore and offshore in the Caspian Sea. These are home to an estimated 7 percent of the world's proven natural gas reserves and 3 percent of proven oil reserves. Most of these resources are found in Kazakhstan, Turkmenistan, and Uzbekistan. Tajikistan and Kyrgyzstan have large potential for generating hydro-electric power.

    Central Asia is thus of prime importance in India's energy security policy. Over the past decade, India's state-owned Oil and Natural Gas Corporation (ONGC) has sought to invest in Kazakhstan, which has three of the world's richest oilfields. ONGC acquired sizeable stakes in the Alibekmola and Kurmangazy oilfields in Kazakh-owned areas of the Caspian Sea. However, although the Indian Government has begun investing in oil fields in Central Asia, its policy on how to transport this oil to the Indian market or work out oil swap deals is still evolving.

3. India has opportunity to exploit the uranium resources of CAR's. Among CARs, Kazakhstan and Uzbekistan are major producers of uranium, producing 20 percent of the world.[120] Kazakhstan is second

---

[120]   British Biological Survey (2012).

largest producer accounting 14 percent and Uzbekistan is eighth producer accounting 6 percent of total. These countries will play vital role in this area and is expected to increase its production.[121]

4. Uzbekistan offers investment opportunity in gold, cotton and gas. The government of this country provides cordial environment for investment like duty-free imported capital goods and tax holidays. Uzbekistan has changed its industrial policy after 2000, wherein only mining, machinery manufacturing and agriculture listed under public undertakings. These opportunities positively affect small and medium size industries as well as agriculture, which the policy makers of India, realize and believe that the CAR's are important due to its strategic location[122]. For increasing the relationship, revival of traditional linkages with Central Asia and with other neighbouring countries have primary importance for India.[123]

5. There are other significant potential areas for expanding mutually beneficial partnership between the two sides. With the partnership between India and CARs getting stronger, it becomes necessary for both sides to identify future areas of strategic cooperation. Currently, the areas of mutual interest include infrastructure, information technology, telecommunication sector, science and technology, knowledge industries such as pharmaceuticals and biotechnology and education and healthcare. India has signed number of agreements with this region which envisages cooperation in the field of healthcare, medical services and pharmacy. Besides India needs establishment of direct cooperation in joint scientific research, visits of experts and

---

[121] T. Kassenova. (2010). Uranium Production and Nuclear Energy in Central Asia: assessment of Security Challenges and Risks, China and Eurasia Forum Quarterly, 8 (2): 223.

[122] K. Kak. (2005). 'India's Strategic and Security Interest in Central Asia'. *In:* V. Nagendra Rao and Mohammad Monir Alam (eds.), *Central Asia: Present Challenges and Future Prospects*. New Delhi: Knowledge World, p. 207.

[123] Speech of Indian Defence Minister, Mr. Pranab Mukherjee, available at http// www. indiaembassy.org/press_release/2005/june.

specialists, exchange of information in the field of health services and medicine.

6. India has tremendous potential of investment in the agriculture sector of CARs, where huge cultivable area is still not fully utilised. Since India has very high experiences in agricultural sector, it can play a significant role in this sector of CARs.

7. Central Asian States are going through a major construction boom. Housing and commercial spaces as well as infrastructure up-gradation are all taking place simultaneously. Several overseas entities as well as many local companies are participating in this very lucrative activity. However, there is not a single Indian construction company, which has a presence in this field.

8. Tourism is another important area where India and CAR's can strengthen their relations. It can bring substantial income and promote interconnectedness between the two regions, having common and contiguous borders, climate continuity, similar geographical features and age-old relations.

Challenges

India has difficult task ahead before it can successfully exploit these opportunities with CAR's. Though India and CAR's have age-old relationship and with the signing of trade agreements, and MoU's since 1996, much of the problems seem to have been resolved. Still there remains number of challenges, which are difficult to be resolved and could not be isolated from the social, political, ideological and economic factors of these nations. Looking at the current trade level between these two regions, the trend is not in desired direction. Following are some of the major problems that stand in the way of carrying trade and commerce at optimal level.

1. The CARs as virgin market has become one of the major targets of the global economic giants. Many developed and technology efficient

developing countries are vying to gain upper hand in capturing this market. As such, the level of efficiency and competition is very high. This directly and indirectly hinders India's progress in this region. Consequently, India has not been able to become an important player in Central Asia, both in the strategic and economic domains. It is not in a position to play equal with the "big four" (Russia, China, the United States, the European Union), and its influence cannot even be compared to that of Turkey or Iran, or even to that of South Korea or Japan. India's presence in this region is minimal as compared to these countries. In this context, for Indian traders who want to sell goods in this region, a considerable market research is inevitable to ensure suitability of product in these markets. Advertising and sales promotion also needs to be carried simultaneously.

2. Lack of direct connectivity with CAR's is another challenge for bilateral trade and economic cooperation. The absence of an efficient transport link between India and CAR's mainly explains for the huge gulf between the potential trade and actual trade between the two regions. India's overland access to CAR's is through Pakistan and Afghanistan, but instability in Afghanistan and Pakistan's not-willing-approach remains major obstacle in the way of realizing large trade and commerce potential between the two regions. This also hampers the growth of other potential sectors like tourism and development of pipeline infrastructure such as TAPI and IPI, which could have otherwise provided another option to improve India's relations with the CAR's.

3. The quantum of financial infrastructure to support trade for India in the region is miserably low in absolute and comparative terms. The same is the case for the CARs. There are only representative offices of Punjab National Bank and State Bank of India in this region, while no bank from this region has yet began its operations in India. Presently many Indian companies like Punj Lloyd, ONGC Videsh Limited (OVL), GAIL etc. in different fields of productive activities in the region are

facing money transaction problems. Currently, Indian EXIM bank is the only active institution, which have established network with National Export-Import Insurance Company and National Bank for Foreign Economic Activity of Uzbekistan. Although this EXIM bank uses high efforts to develop economic cooperation with CARs, alone is not enough to deepen its relations and not able to compete with western institutes. As such efforts with all earnestness to foster financial infrastructure should be initiated by both the regions.

4. Both India and CAR's charge custom duties on imports to protect their home industries. Similarly, tariff rates are put on exports of raw materials. Importers and exporters are also required to fulfil several customs formalities and rules. Moreover, foreign trade policy procedures, rules and regulations differ from country to country in CARs and keep on changing from time to time.

5. The producers and traders across the regions suffer acute lack of information with regard to each other's markets and products. As such this becomes an important barrier for the growth of trade between the regions. There are least arrangements for trade fairs between the regions which could make up for the gaps in information. Absence of trade fairs leaves the economic ties between the regions at unchanged.

6. Another problem pertains to the unfavourable trade balance on the part of CAR's. There could be many factors responsible for this imbalance but the prominent one may include an inability to compete in the Indian market on the grounds of quality, price, supply capability etc. Thus it is understandable that unless sizable exports from CARs find a stable market in India, the magnitude of the trade imbalance cannot be reduced.

7. Frequent changes in the rules and regulations regarding standards and certification create many difficulties for the producers and traders. It takes relatively a fair amount of time to find a place in the market for the goods and articles. Once a product creates market for it, a

change in the rules may make it ineligible thereby creating enormous difficulties for the producers. It has been frequently noted that the rules, procedures and duties are revised through the government budget on the one hand, and the provisions of the trade and transit treaties on the other. Such types of changes and modifications create confusions among the business communities, which ultimately affects the transactions in a great deal.

8. Trade is an activity carried between two parties, requires a certain degree of good faith and understanding. On the other hand, it demands mutual cooperation. The bilateral trade between India and CAR's depends much on the bilateral agreements on trade. At the official level as well as commercial level the respective governments fail to initiate and foster an environment of trust between different stakeholders. As such few breakthroughs in the development of bilateral trade are visible in the past.

9. Different languages and scripts in Central Asian countries is also a problem for facing business people from India. Price lists and catalogues are prepared in local languages. Advertisements and correspondence also are to be done in local languages. A trader wishing to buy or sell goods abroad must know their language. This hinders smooth flow of information fundamental for trade and investment.

10. India has yet to create influential space in important regional organisations. The Conference on Interaction and Confidence Building Measures in Asia (CICA) is the only organization in which both India and CARs are members. This was initiated by Kazakhstan to broaden network for security through involving both CARs and Asian countries, but it has still a long way to go to solve many problems of the region including extremism. Similarly, SAARC, which also seek to build security environment of South Asian countries, has not taken-off as per expectations.

On the basis of aforementioned, it can be summed up that the intensive competition among major powers hinders India's progress in this region. Similarly, custom duties, changing rules and regulations etc were seen major problems by both regions in their own perspective. Equally, weak growth of supportive financial services and lack of information network to facilitate trade and investment is problem for growing economic relations. Subsequently, India as an immediate neighbour has major geostrategic and economic interest in the region but economic and political stability in CARs, Pakistan and Afghanistan seem to be the most crucial factor to gain access. Similarly, interests of India are influenced by the geostrategic policies of China, Russia and Iran. Therefore, Indian, "Look Central Asian Policy" depends upon the regional complex. In order to accomplish this project a "cooperative framework of inclusive engagement" would be optimal solution. Equally, India could exploit its interest through joining regional cooperation's, which Central Asian States are keenly focusing to set up with different nations. These co-operations could reduce the problems and enable India to utilize the trade and energy potential of this landlocked region.

CHAPTER 8

Conclusions

Trade has a vital role in cementing and enhancing the relations between the countries. More they trade, more would be they involved with each other, and the more they get involved, more benefits and responsibilities they have to share. Since Central Asian countries are in the immediate neighbourhood of India, deep relations with this region are therefore, an urgency. The relationship between the two regions has economic as well as strategic values. Though India and Central Asian region had rich historical and cultural relations, but with the growth of nation states along the globe and disintegration of the former USSR, such closeness got impacted. Hence, in this fast age of market economic system, the development of connections particularly through sea, air and electronic communications, have offered the opportunities to countries and continents, which are far away from each other, to come closer and take advantages from their economic resources and prosperity. In the context of deep cultural, historical and social links with Central Asia, India's "Look North Policy", would benefit both the regions. Particularly CAR's rich hydrocarbon reserves and precious and strategic metals offer an opportunity to India, which in turn has a lot of consumer goods and technology to offer to Central Asian markets. Trade has therefore, a lot of significance in this regard.

Policy planners in both India and CAR's after 1991 employed variety of means to foster bilateral trade. India particularly has been serious about the opportunities of developing closer, long-term ties with this region. High level visits were exchanged, in an effort to develop and foster economic ties and in the due course of time, several agreements and MoU's were signed, and framed with greater prospects, and comprehensiveness, which has facilitated economic relations with larger scope for mutual benefits.

The Gravity Model employed in the present study determined the impact of the variables such as distance, gross national income and percent capita income on trade between India and Central Asia states for the period 2000-2012. The result shows significant value, that 1 percent increase in the size of GNI of given country would increase bilateral trade by 0.626 percent. Similarly, the coefficient of distance shows that when trade falls by 1.6 percent for every 1 percent increase in the distance between them and vice-versa. Therefore, both coefficients are empirically reliable with.

In predicted trade potential of India and CAR's through Gravity Model equation, the ratio (P/A) shows that India has adequate potential to enhance its trade with this region. Results are also indicative that India's actual bilateral trade with Central Asian countries is below than the potential. Precisely, in order to realize the opportunity of enhancing the trade as evident from the difference between actual and estimated trade, trade promotional policies like increase in GNI and reduction in transport costs needs to be adopted. In addition, the North-South Transport Corridor project has potential to decrease transport costs. This corridor connects can't connect only India and Central Asian countries but European countries and Russia to Indian Ocean, the Persian Gulf and South Asian States. Similarly, the Trans-Asian Highway, Transport Corridor Europe Caucasus Asia and Asian Highway can link Asian nations with Europe. It is expected that with the possibility of these projects, there would be increase in bilateral economic relations.

India-CAR's trade has provided scope for a number of items to be included in the trade nomenclature. In the process of the development of trade, the commodity structure has not changed. From the beginning, India's major export to CAR's includes tea, coffee, salt. Same is the case with CAR's which export traditional goods to India and no changes have been seen in the composition. However, there are many commodities in which trade could be increased. Based on the Revealed Comparative Advantage Index, results show that India has RCA >1 in several items, thereby implying that India could increase export to CAR's. Chemicals and pharmaceuticals (HS-30) are among the items that have export potential to Central Asian States and are among major export items from India to this region. During 2009-12, India exported US$ 308.01 million of chemicals and pharmaceuticals products to CARs, accounting 31.01 percent of India's total exports to this region. There are other export potential items related with (HS 30) such as carbonates (HS-2836), animal and human blood for therapeutic uses (HS-3002), medicaments (HS-3004) and fungicides, herbicides and insecticides (HS-3808).

Equally, Coffee and Tea (HS-09) has export potential to CARs, but currently it is marginally exported. During 2000-03, India exported coffee and tea worth US$ 62.38 million, accounting 26.25 percent of the total trade with CARs however, during 2009-12, its share declined to 13.7 percent, meaning thereby that the potential of this item is not being explored. Some other items including in this category are cream and milk concentrated (HS-0402), vegetable saps (HS-1302), oils (animal or vegetables HS-1516), and sugar confectionary (HS-1704). Cotton products (HS-61) also stand on the list of commodities that have good trade potential. India's export of cotton products to Kazakhstan, Kyrgyzstan and Tajikistan increased from US$ 14.01 million, accounting 5.9 percent of total trade in 2000-03 to US$73.86 million in 2003-06, accounting 15 percent of total trade with CAR's.

Based on the Revealed Comparative Advantages Index, Machinery and transport equipment are the largest in the import basket of CARs, hence a major potential sector for India to ponder over As of now, these countries mainly import these commodities from Russia, China, Germany, US and Ukraine. Other items including in this category are refrigerators and freezers (HS-8418), air vacuum pumps (HS-8414), pumps for liquids (HS-8413), laboratory equipments (HS-8419), machines and mechanical appliances (HS-8473), transistors (HS-8524), wires and cables (HS-8544), public transport motor vehicles (HS-8702), motor cars (HS-8703), spare parts and other accessories (HS-8708). Lead ores and concentrates, petroleum products, cosmetics, soaps and organic products, plastic articles, rubber articles and medical and surgical products are the other export potential items to CARs.

Similarly, Central Asia States has RCA >1 in many export items to India. Since 1996, India's imports from CAR increased steadily. The export potential items of CARs to India includes: natural and cultured pearls or semi precious stones (HS-71), zinc and articles (HS-79), salt, sulphur, earth and stone, plastering materials, lime, and cement (HS-25), inorganic chemicals, organic and inorganic compounds of precious metals (HS-28), lead and articles (HS-78), nuclear reactors, boilers, machinery mechanical appliances parts (HS-84) and iron and steel (HS-72), flat-rolled products of iron (HS- 7208), ferrous-alloys (HS-7202), iron and steel rods (HS-7214), tubes (HS-7304), and pipes (HS-7305).

Correspondingly, there exists an immense future prospect for India and CAR's cooperation in many sectors like: banking, construction, information technology, pharmaceuticals etc. They have comparative advantage in various commodities and if trade relations between two regions enhance, large benefits will be shared by the participating countries.

The economic development of India primarily depends upon the availability of adequate energy resources. As argued by India's current Prime Minister and leading economist Dr. Manmohan Singh, "Energy security is second only in our scheme of things to food security". Therefore securing an uninterrupted and adequate supply of energy is critical for keeping India's economic wheels in motion. Currently India imports seventy percent of its oil supply from abroad and is expected to become ever more reliant on imported energy. In this respect cultivating alternative sources of energy supply has become a vital concern for India. Central Asian republics can prove to be one of such alternative supply sources.

The richness of the CAR's energy resources came to limelight over the years since the mid-1990s and because of the optimistic energy numbers, it is called a "strategic region". On global level, the CAR's are considered the next oil and gas frontier, where proven oil reserves are between 15 billion to 31 billion barrels, which accounts 2.7 percent of world reserves. Similarly, proven natural gas reserves are at 230 to 360 trillion cubic feet comprising 7 percent of the world reserves. Characteristically Kazakhstan, Turkmenistan and Uzbekistan are considered among world leaders in natural gas production.[124]

Apart from hydrocarbon resources, CARs are blessed with uranium wealth, which is distributed throughout the world unevenly than oil and gas. Access to the uranium reserves in the coming future will became strategically important issue in providing global energy security. In CARs, Kazakhstan and Uzbekistan are major producers of uranium, producing 20 percent of the world. Kazakhstan is however, second largest producer accounting 14 percent and Uzbekistan is eighth producer accounting 6 percent of world total.

There are, however, certain bottlenecks in the way of realizing the vast trade potential existing between the two regions. The impediments are mainly in the form of lack of direct overland connectivity, competition from the global players present in the region, India which needs this region, has to be very innovative and frame a novel strategy to deal with the region in the context of trade and investment

Policy Implications

As follows from above discussion, India and CAR's have many potential areas for economic cooperation, but simultaneously there are certain hurdles, the pressure of these challenges has affected these countries variedly. However, despite these constrains and keeping in view the existing trade potential between the two regions and a growing energy demand of India, policy planners, political as well as economic analysts in India have to join their minds together to develop a strategy so that these countries of this region will come close because for India, the region has special significance due to its strategic location and energy resources. Based on the conclusions drawn from the study, the following policy recommendation, if given consideration can go long-way in developing and deepen the relations between India and Central Asian States by way of enhancing economic and trade relations.

---

[124] Oil & Gas Journal, 2010

1. India should uphold a selective export policy towards Central Asian States. Having a strong industrial base and human capital accounting 80 percent of the gross regional product in South Asia, India should increase trade concession with Central Asian States-including unilaterally eliminating tariff and non-tariff barriers.

2. Bilateral commission should be established to oversee India's economic relations with its neighbouring countries, with focus on addressing tariff and non-tariff barriers, implementations of trade agreements etc. India-Central Asia free trade forum should be formed, comprising academia, business organization, members of private sector and media to scrutinize this commission. Moreover give each other the status of the *most favoured nation* and arrange more international trade fairs.

3. Both India and Central Asian States should design comprehensive trade policies with strategic focus. Both should formulate measures that promote open economic relationship.

4. The unfavourable relationship between India and Pakistan is a major impediment to continental trade across Eurasia, which needs to be smoothened.

5. India, China, and the Central Asian Republics should develop a sub-regional framework agreement designed to facilitate cross-border transit trade along the measures adopted by Association for South-East Nations, Greater Mekong Sub-region, Transport Corridor Europe-Caucasus, and others.

6. Rebuild Afghanistan's transport network, which can prove indispensable for connectivity to Central Asian States.

7. Enhance and develop relations between existing and newly formed financial institutions and banking agencies.

8. Create a consortium for development of information technology.

9. Build partnership and complementary co-operation in sectors of comparative advantage.

10. India should find spaces in regional economic and political forums.

Directions for further studies

Present book makes a modest attempt towards the study of trade relations between India and Central Asia republics. Keeping in view the scope of the subject, there is a need of more research to be carried out. Firstly, given the theoretical ground of the present study and as for as application of gravity model is concerned, it is suggested that future research works could also endeavour to take into account the transportation costs embedding it in the gravity coefficient. Equally the studies of bilateral trade can incorporate further variables to grasp hold of fluctuations of bilateral trade and on the availability of more data at disaggregate level, could inform their empirical analysis by pondering over domains such as industry.

For the application of gravity model to determination of FDI, there is a possibility of incorporating factor endowments like ratios of capital to labour and of land to labour and schooling level rather than holding a simple basket of dummy variables. Variables like unemployment rate, relative wage, population density, investment density, and employment openness, number of skill workers, macroeconomic stability, and extended market size could be introduced to the model to ascertain the key driver of locational choice.

Moreover, further research works could also evaluate the complete system consisting of bilateral export equations and bilateral FDI equations between India and Central Asia alongside as both FDI and trade appear to be depended on the identical set of variables. Nevertheless, one must also keep in mind the concurrent causality between the two.

BIBLIOGRAPHY

Acharya and Shankar (2008). *India's Macroeconomic Performance and Policies since 2000*, Working Paper No. 225, Indian Council for Research on International Economic Relations (ICRIER), New Delhi.

Adams T. (2004). 'Caspian Energy Development'. *In:* Akiner S. (eds.), *The Caspian: Politics, Energy and Security*. New York: Routledge, pp.79-96.

Ahmad S. and Ghani E. (2007). South Asia's Growth and Regional Integration: An Overview, in *South Asia: Growth and Regional Integration*, World Bank, Washington, DC.

Ahmad T. (2009). 'Geopolitics of West Asian and Central Asian oil and gas: Implication for India's Energy Security'. *In:* Noronha L. and Sudarshan A. (eds.), *India's Energy Security*. London: Routledge, pp.64-86.

Ahmad T. (2010). 'Geopolitics of Central Asia's Oil and Gas Resources Implications for India's Energy Security'. *In:* Kaw M. and Gleason G. (eds.), *Central Asia in Retrospect and Prospect*. New Delhi: Readworthy, pp.133-148.

Akhanov S. and Buranbayeva L. (1996). 'Foreign Investment and Trade in Kazakhstan'. *In:* Kaminski B. (eds.), *Economic Transition in Russia and the New States of Eurasia*. New York: M. E. Sharpe, pp. 138-158.

Alam M. (2004). 'Central Asian Republics Quest for Security in the Post-Soviet Period'. *In:* Warikoo K. and Singh M. (eds.), *Central Asian Since Independence.* Kolkata: Shipra Publication, pp.106-139.

Amin A. and Ainekova D. (2012). The Long Run Growth Rate of the Kazakhstan's Economy, *Eurasian Journal of Business and Economics.* 5(9): 45-46.

Anderson J. (1979). A Theoretical Foundation for the Gravity Equation, *American Economic Review.* 69(1):106-116.

Anderson J. (2010). 'The Incidence of Gravity'. *In:* Bergeijk A. and Brakman (eds.), *The Gravity Model in International Trade: Advances and Applications.* UK: Cambridge University Press, pp. 71-87.

Anderson J. and Wincoop E. (2001). Border, Trade and Welfare, Working paper No. 508, Department of Economics, Boston College.

Asopa K. (2006). India's Stakes in Central Asia: An Appraisal of India's Central Asia Policy, in *Struggle for Sphers of Interest in Trans-Caucasia-Central Asia and India's Stakes.* New Delhi: Manak Publications, pp. 285-318.

Auty R. (2008). 'Improving the Beneficial Socio-Economic Impact of Hydrocarbon Extraction on Local/Regional development in Caspian Economies. *In:* Najman B., Pomfret R. and Raballand G. (eds.), *The Economic and Politics of oil in the Caspian Basin.* Newyork: Routledge, pp. 159-175.

Babak V. (1999). 'Kazakhstan: Big Politics Around Oil'. *In:* Croissant M. and Aras B. (eds.), *Oil and Geopolitics in the Caspian Sea Region.* London Praeger, pp 181-208.

Bahgat G. (2006). Central Asia and Energy Security, *Asian Affairs*, Vol. xxxvii, No. 1, pp. 1-16.

Baltagi H. (2000). *Econometric Analysis of Panel Data*, Chapter 14, Englewood Cliffs, Prentice-Hall.

Barry M. (2009). Foreign Direct Investment in Central Asian Energy: A CGE Model, *Eurasian Journal of Business and Economics*. 2(3): 35-54.

Batra A. (2004). *India's Global Potential: The Gravity Model approach*, Working Paper No. 151, Indian Council For Research on International Economic Relations (ICRIER), New Delhi.

Batra A. and Khan Z. (2005). *Revealed Comparative Advantage: An Analysis for India and China*, Working Paper No. 168, Indian Council for Research on International Economic Relations (ICRIER), New Delhi.

Bek-Ali Y.K. (2007). 'Kazakhstan-India Trade and Economic Relations'. *In:* Santhanam, Baizakova and Dwivedi (eds.), *India-Kazakhstan Perspective: Regional and International Interactions*. New Delhi: Anamaya Publishers, pp. 40-47.

Benedictis L. and Taglioni D. (2011). 'The Gravity Model in International Trade'. *In:* Benedictis L. and Salvatici L (eds.), *The Trade Impact of European Union Preferential Policies: An analysis Through Gravity Models*. Germany: Springer, pp. 55-88.

Bergstrand J. (1985). The Gravity Equation in International Trade: Some Microeconomic Foundations and Empirical Evidence, Review of Economics and Statistics. 67(3): 474-481.

Bergstrand J. (1989). The Generalized Gravity Equation, Monopolistic Competition and The Factor-Proportions Theory in International Trade, *Review of Economics and Statistics*. 71(1):143-153.

Bergstrand J. (1990). The Heckscher-Ohlin-Samuelson Model, the Linder Hypothesis and the Determinants of Bilateral Intra-Industry Trade, Economic Journal. 100(403):1216-1253.

Bergstrand J. and Egger P. (2010). 'A General Equilibrium Theory for Estimating Gravity Equations of Bilateral FDI, final goods trade and intermediate trade flows'. *In:* Bergeijk A. and Brakman (eds.), *The Gravity Model in International Trade: Advances and Applications.* UK: Cambridge University Press, pp. 29-70.

Bhatia K. (2013). 'Indo-Central Asian Relations: Challenges and Prospects'. *In:* Mir M. (eds.), *Globalizing Eurasia: Potential and Challenges.* New Delhi: Mehak Printing Press, pp. 133-148.

Blank S. (2010). 'The Influence of External Actors in Central Asia'. *In:* Emilian K. (eds.), *The New Central Asia: The Regional Impact of International Actors.* Chennai World Scientific, pp. 281-302.

Bosker E. and Garretsen H. (2010). 'Trade costs, market access, and economic geography: why the empirical specification of trade costs matters'. *In:* Bergeijk A. and Brakman (eds.), *The Gravity Model in International Trade: Advances and Applications.* UK: Cambridge University Press, pp.193-223.

Bosworth B. Collins S. and Flaaen A. (2008). *Trading with Asian's Giants,* Working Paper No. 220, Indian Council for Research on International Economic Relations (ICRIER), New Delhi.

Boulhol H. and Serres A. (2010). 'The impact of economic geography on GDP per capita in OECD countries'. *In:* Bergeijk A. and Brakman (eds.), *The Gravity Model in International Trade: Advances and Applications.* UK: Cambridge University Press, pp. 323-354.

Brooks D. (2010). 'Regional Cooperation, Infrastructure and trade Costs in Asia'. *In:* Stone S. (eds.), Trade Facilitation and Regional Cooperation in Asia. USA: Edward Elgar, pp. 1-20.

Chandra A. (2009). Geopolitics of Central Asian Energy Resources and Indian Interest, *Journal of Peace Studies.* 16(1-2). Available on http://www.icpsnet. org/adm/pdf/1251369051.pdf (accessed 26 January 2012)

Chenoy A. (2007). 'Oil Politics of Central Asia and Caspian Sea Basin: The US Game Plan'. *In:* Anuradha M. and Patnaik A. (eds.), *Commonwealth of Independent States: Energy, Security and Development.* New Delhi Knowledge World, pp.113-130.

Chrystal K. (1998). 'International Monetary Arrangements and International Trade: Does the Monetary Regime Matter'. *In:* Cook G. (eds.), *The Economics and Politics of International trade.* New York: Routledge, pp. 42-52.

Crandall S. (2006). Caspian Energy: Prospects, Pipelines and Problems in *Energy, Economics and Politics in the Caspian Region.* London: Praeger Security International, pp. 9-54.

Dash P. (2000). 'Oil Transport and Trade: Dilemmas and Options Facing Kazakhstan and Turkmenistan'. *In:* Shamas-din (eds.), *Geopolitics and Energy Resources in Central Asia and Caspian Sea Region.* New Delhi: Lancer Books, pp. 71-90.

Delay J. (1999). 'The Caspian Oil Pipeline tangle: A Steel Web of Confusion'. *In:* Croissant M. and Aras B. (eds.), *Oil and Geopolitics in the Caspian Sea Region.* London: Praeger, pp. 43-82.

Dikkaya M. and Keles I. (2006). A case study of foreign direct investment in Kyrgyzstan, *Central Asian Survey.* 25(1-2): 149-156.

Dosumov Rustam (1996). 'Uzbekistan: A National Path to the Market'. *In:* Rumer Boris (eds.), *Central Asia in Transition: Dilemmas of Political and Economic Development.* London: M. E. Sharpe, pp. 136-197.

Dwivedi R. (2008). 'India-Uzbekistan Relations: Prospects for Cooperation'. *In:* Dash P. (eds.), *Emerging Asia in Focus: Issues and Problems.* Delhi: Academic Excellence, pp. 348-364.

Ehteshami A. (2004). 'Geopolitics of Hydrocarbons in Central and Western Asia'. *In:* Akiner S. (eds.), *The Caspian: Politics, Energy and Security.* New York Routledge, pp. 55-67.

Esentugelov A. (1998). 'Kazakhstan: The Prospects and Perils of Foreign Investment'. *In:* Rumer B. and Zhukov S. (eds.), *Central Asia: The Challenges of Independence.* New York M. E. Sharpe, pp. 237-258.

Farrukh and Yunus (2012). Who is Trading Well in Central Asia: A gravity Analysis of Exports from the Regional Powers to the Region, *Eurasian Journal of Business and Economics.* 5(9): 21-43.

Fedorov G. Boris (1995). 'Macroeconomic Policy and Stabilisation in Russia'. *In:* Aslund Andren (eds.), *Russian Economic Reforms at Risk.* London Pinter Publishers, pp. 9-18.

Felipe J. and Kumar U. (2010). *The Role of Trade Facilitation in Central Asia: A Gravity Model,* Working Paper No. 628, Asian Development Bank.

Fumagalli M. (2010). 'The United States and Central Asia'. *In:* Emilian K. (eds.), *The New Central Asia: The Regional Impact of International Actors.* Chennai World Scientific, pp. 177-190.

Gidadhubli G. (2000). 'Economics and Politics of Caspian Energy Resources'. *In:* Shamas-din (eds.), *Geopolitics and Energy Resources in Central Asia and Caspian Sea Region.* New Delhi: Lancer Books, pp. 91-106.

Gidadhubli G. (2006). 'Regional Cooperation in Central Asia: Performance, Prospects and Challenges'. *In:* Santhanam K. and Sultanov K. (eds.), *India-Kazakhstan Relations: Enhancing the Partnership.* New Delhi Anamaya Publishers, pp. 77-94.

Gidadhubli G. (2008). 'Central Asian States Transition to Market Economy'. *In:* Dash P. (eds.), *Emerging Asia in Focus: Issues and Problems.* Delhi Academic Excellence, pp. 392-405.

Gilbert J. and Banik N. (2010). 'Regional Integration and Trade Costa in South Asia'. *In:* Stone S. (eds.), Trade Facilitation and Regional Cooperation in Asia.USA: Edward Elgar, pp. 123-155.

Gleason G. (2003). Economic and Political Reform, in *Market and Politics in Central Asia: Structural Reform and Political Change.* New York: Routledge, pp. 1-19.

Gleason G. (2003). Kazakhstan and Globalization, in *Market and Politics in Central Asia: Structural Reform and Political Change.* New York: Routledge, pp. 37-64.

Goldberg I., Branstetter L. and Goddard G. (2008). *Globalization and Technology Absorption in Europe and Central Asia: The Role of Trade, FDI and Cross-Border Knowledge Flows,* Policy Research Working Paper No. 150. The World Bank, Washington.

Gopal S. (2005). The Role of Indo-Central Asian Relations in Making a New Asia, in *Dialogue and Understanding Central Asia and India: The Soviet and the Post-Soviet Era.* New Delhi: Shipra Publication, pp. 155-179.

Granville Brigtte (1995). 'Farewell Ruble Zone'. *In:* Aslund Andren (eds.), *Russian Economic Reforms at Risk.* London Pinter Publishers, pp. 66-88.

Hiestand T. (2005). Using Pooled Model, Random Model and Fixed Model Multiple Regression To Measure Foreign Direct Investment in Taiwan, *International Business and Economic Research Journal.* 4(12): 37-52.

Huchet J. (2010). 'India and China in Central Asia: Mirroring Their Bilateral Relations'. *In:* Laruelle, Huchet F., Peyrouse S. and Balci B. (eds.), *China and India in Central Asia: A New Great Game.* UK: Palgrave Maclillan, pp. 81-97.

Hunter S. (1996). Central Asia and Its Neighbors, in *Central Asia Since Independence.* London: Praeger, pp. 124-146.

Hunter S. (1996). Economic Revitalization and Reforms, in *Central Asia Since Independence*. London: Praeger, pp. 66-87.

Hyman A. (1994). 'Central Asia's Relations with Afghanistan and South Asia'. *In:* Ferdinand P. (eds.), *The New Central Asia and its Neighbors*. London: The Royal Institute of International Affairs, pp. 75-96.

Ipek P. (2007). The role of oil and gas in Kazakhstan's foreign policy: Looking east or west, *Europe-Asia Studies*. 59(7): 1179-1199.

Jafar M. (2004). 'Kazakhstan: Oil, Politics and the new Great Game'. *In:* Akiner S. (eds.), *The Caspian: Politics, Energy and Security*. New York Routledge, pp.180-197.

JenKun F. (2010). Reassessing a New Great Game between India and China in Central Asia, *China and Eurasia Forum Quarterly*. 8(1): 17-22.

Joshi N. (2006). 'An Appraisal of China's Policy Towards Central Asia'. *In:* Santhanam K. and Sultanov K. (eds.), *India-Kazakhstan Relations: Enhancing the Partnership*. New Delhi: Anamaya Publishers, pp. 64-76.

Kamal Y., Khan M. and Muhayudin A. (2012). Pakistan's Trade Potential in ECO Countries: Prospects and Challenges, *Asian Journal of Business and Management Sciences*. 1(7): 60-67.

Kapparov K. (2012). Kazakhstan's Investment in Central Asia, Working Paper No. 14, Institute of Public Policy and Administration.

Kavalski E. (2010). Introduction: Framing India's International Interactions, in *India and Central Asia: The Mythmaking and International Relations of a Rising power*. New York: I. B. Tauris Publishers, pp. 1-20.

Kavalski E. (2010). 'Uncovering the New Central Asia: The Dynamics of External Agency in a Turbulent Region'. *In:* Emilian K. (eds.), *The New*

Central Asia: The Regional Impact of International Actors. Chennai World Scientific, pp.1-26.

Kavalski E. (2010). The Look North Policy: Uncovering india's Discourses on Central Asia, *India and Central Asia: The Mythmaking and International Relations of a Rising power.* New York: I. B. Tauris Publishers, pp. 79-110.

Kaw M. (2009). Restoring India's Silk Route Links with South and Central Asia across Kashmir: Challenges and opportunities, *China and Eurasia Forum Quarterly.* 7(2):59-74.

Kepaptsoglou K., Karlaftis M. and Tsamboulas D. (2010). The Gravity Model Specification for Modeling International Trade Flows and Free Trade Agreement Effects: A 10-Year Review of Empirical Studies, *The Open Economics Journal,* 3(20):1-13.

Khasanova M. (1998). 'Kazakhstan: Foreign Trade Policy'. *In:* Rumer B. and Zhukov S. (eds.), Central Asia: The Challenges of Independence. New York: M. E. Sharpe, pp.169-207.

Knight W. and Bhatia V. (2010). 'The United Nations and Central Asia'. *In:* Emilian K. (eds.), *The New Central Asia: The Regional Impact of International Actors.* Chennai World Scientific, pp. 89-114.

Koichuev T. (1996). 'Kyrgyzstan: Economic Crisis and Transition Strategy'. *In:* Rumer B. (eds.), *Central Asia in Transition: Dilemmas of Political and Economic Development.* New York: M. E. Sharpe, pp. 166-197.

Krugman P. (1998). 'Ricardo's Difficult Idea: Why Intellectuals Don't Understand Comparative Advantage'. *In:* Cook G. (eds.), *The Economics and Politics of International trade.* New York: Routledge, pp. 22-36.

Kulipanova E. (2012). *International Transport in Central Asia: Understanding the Patterns of (Non-) Cooperation,* Working Paper No. 2 Institute of Public Policy and Administration.

Kumar N. (2006). *Emerging Multinationals: Trends, Patterns and Determinanta of Outward Investment by Indian Enterprises*, Working Paper No. 117, Research and Information System for Developing Countries (RIS), New Delhi.

Laruelle M. (2010). 'Russia Facing China and India in Central Asia: Cooperation, Competition and Hesitations'. *In:* Laruelle, Huchet F., Peyrouse S. and Balci B. (eds.), *China and India in Central Asia: A New Great Game.* UK: Palgrave Maclillan, pp. 9-24.

Laxmi V. (2007). India-Central Asia Relations: Quest for Energy Security, *Dialogue.* 8(4):174-183.

Lewin M. (2008). 'The Impact of Oil Revenue on Economic Performance: Analytical Issues'. *In:* Najman B., Pomfret R. and Raballand G. (eds.), *The Economic and Politics of oil in the Caspian Basin.* Newyork: Routledge, pp. 30-42.

Liuhto K. and Kaartemo V. (2011). 'Special Economic Zones in Russia: Can They Lead to an Economic Boom Similar to the Chinese'. *In:* Marinov M and Marinova S. (eds.), *The Changing Nature of Doing Business in Transition Economies.* New York Palgrave Macmillan, pp. 104-118.

Luong P. (2002). Sources of Change: The Transitional Context in Central Asia, in *Institutional Change and Political Continuity in Post-Soviet Central Asia.* UK: Cambridge University Press, pp. 102-155.

M. Irina. (2011). 'Russia's Energy Policy in Central Asia Imperatives for India'. *In:* K. Warikoo (eds.), *Central Asia and South Asia: Energy Cooperation and Transport Linkages.* New Delhi: Pentagon Press, pp. 59-67.

Mahalingam S. (2004). 'India and Central Asia Energy Cooperation'. *In:* Santhanam K. and Dwivedi R. (eds.), *India and Central Asia: Advancing the Common Interest.* New Delhi: Anamaya Publishers, pp. 111-143.

Manoharan N. and Bhonsle R. (2011). 'India: Afghanistan's Partner in Nation-Building'. in Sawhney, Sahgal and Kanwal (eds.), Afghanistan: A Role for India. New Delhi: Knowledge World, pp. 163-188.

Mavlonov I. (2006). India's Economic Diplomacy with Central Asian Nations and the Economic Development of the Region, *Dialogue.* 7(3): 24-42.

Mavlonov I. (2007). 'India's Economic Diplomacy Trends with Central Asia: The Potential and Priorities'. *In:* Anuradha M. and Patnaik A. (eds.), *Commonwealth of Independent States: Energy, Security and Development.* New Delhi Knowledge World, pp. 279-296.

Mesamed V. (1999). 'Turkmenistan: Oil, Gas and Caspian Politics'. *In:* Croissant M. and Aras B. (eds.), Oil and Geopolitics in the Caspian Sea Region. London Praeger, pp. 209-226.

Misra A. (2007). 'Contours of India's Energy Security: Harmonising Domestic and External Options'. *In:* Wesley M. (eds.), *Energy Security in Asia.* London Routledge, pp. 68-88.

Morita K. (2011). 'EU Enlargement and Inward FDI in Central Europe: An Evolutionary Game Approach'. *In:* Marinov M and Marinova S. (eds.), *The Changing Nature of Doing Business in Transition Economies.* New York: Palgrave Macmillan, pp. 30-42.

Mukerji A.K. (2006). 'India-Kazakhstan Relations'. *In:* Santhanam K. and Sultanov K. (eds.), *India-Kazakhstan Relations: Enhancing the Partnership.* New Delhi: Anamaya Publishers, pp. 1-9.

Musaeva I. (2008). 'Prospects of Kyrgyzstan-India Economic Cooperation'. *In:* Santhanam K. and Dwivedi R. (eds.), *India-Kyrgyz Relations: Perspective and Prospects.* New Delhi: Anamaya Publishers, pp. 32-46

Nanay J. (2000). The Industry's Race for Caspian Oil Reserves, in *Caspian Energy Resources Implication for the Arab Gulf,* published by The Emirates Centre for Strategic Studies and Research, Abu Dhabi, pp. 111-126.

Nilsson L. (2011). 'European Union Preferential Trading Arrangements: Evolution, Content and Use'. *In:* Benedictis L. and Salvatici L (eds.), *The Trade Impact of European Union Preferential Policies: An analysis Through Gravity Models.* Germany: Springer, pp. 15-31.

Noronha L. (2009). 'India's Energy Security landscape: Joining the dots and looking ahead'. *In:* Noronha L. and Sudarshan A. (eds.), *India's Energy Security.* London: Routledge, pp. 223-233.

Nygren B. (2008). The Regional Organizations of the Russian-led Regional Security Complex, in *The Rebuilding of Greater Russia.* London: Routledge, pp. 24-45.

Olcott M. (2002). Can Kazakhstan Regain Its Promise, in *Kazakhstan: Unfulfilled Promise.* Washington: Carnegie Endownment for International Peace, pp. 214-244.

Olcott M. (2011). 'Central Asia's Oil and Gas Reserves: To Whom Do They Matters'. *In:* Hermann and Linn F. (eds.), *Central Asia and The Caucasus.* Singapore: Sage Publication Asia-Pacific Pvt. Ltd, pp. 95-134.

Oliker O. (2007). Kazakhstan's Security Interests and Their Implications for the US-Kazakh Relationship, *China and Eurasia Forum Quarterly.* 5(2): 63-72.

Panda J. (2009). India's Approach to Central Asia: Strategic Intents and Geo-Political Calculus, *China and Eurasia Forum Quarterly.* 7(3): 103-113.

Pandey K. (2000). 'India and Central Asia: Alternative Trade Routes and Transit Options'. *In:* Shamas-din (eds.), *Geopolitics and Energy Resources in Central Asia and Caspian Sea Region.* New Delhi Lancer Books, pp. 191-202.

Pant G. (2007). Energy security in Asia: The Necessity of Interdependence, *Strategic Analysis.* 31(3): 523-542.

Parida P. and Sahoo P. (2007). Export-led Growth in South Asia: A Panel Cointegration Analysis, *International Economic Journal.* 21(2): 155-175.

Patnaik A. (2012). 'Central Asia as Potential Theatre of Non-Traditional Conflict'. *In:* Shamas-din (eds.), *Geopolitics and Energy Resources in Central Asia and Caspian Sea Region.* New Delhi: Lancer Books, pp. 117-136.

Peyrouse S. (2010). 'Comparing the Economic Involvement of China and India in Post-Soviet Central Asia'. *In:* Laruelle, Huchet F., Peyrouse S. and Balci B. (eds.), *China and India in Central Asia: A New Great Game.* UK: Palgrave Maclillan, pp. 155-172.

Pomfret R. (2006). 'Resource abundance, governance and economic performance in Turkmenistan and Uzbekistan'. *In:* Auty R. and Soysa (eds.), *Energy, Wealth and Governance in the Caucasus and Central Asia: Lesson not Learned.* New York: Routledge, pp. 77-93.

Pomfret R. (2006). The Role of Natural Resources. *In: The Central Asian Economics Since Independence.* UK: Princeton University Press, pp. 143-168.

Pomfret R. (2010). Constructing market-based economies in central Asia: A natural experiment, *The European Journal of Comparative Economics.* 7(2): 449-467.

Pomfret R. (2011). 'Trade and Transport in Central Asia'. *In:* Hermann and Linn F. (eds.), *Central Asia and The Caucasus.* Singapore: Sage Publication Asia-Pacific Pte Ltd, pp. 63-94.

Pomfret R. and Anderson K. (2001). Economic Development Strategies in Central Asia Since 1991, *Asian Studies Review*. 25(2): 185-200

Prabir D. (2009). *Global economic and financial crisis: India's trade potential and future prospects*, Working Paper Series, No. 64, Asia-Pacific Research and Training Network on Trade.

Raballand G., Kunth A., Auty R., (2005). Central Asia's transport cost burden and its impact on trade, *Economic System*, Elsevier. 29(3): 6-31.

Rennikova Oksana (1996). 'Transitional Corporation in Central Asia'. *In:* Rumer Boris (eds.), *Central Asia in Transition: Dilemmas of Political and Economic Development*. London:M. E. Sharpe, pp. 67-105.

Roy M. (2001). 'North-South Corridor: Prospective and Challenges for India'. *In:* K. Warikoo (eds.), *Central Asia and South Asia: Energy Cooperation and Transport Linkages*. New Delhi: Pentagon Press, pp. 222-239.

Roy M. (2001). India's Interest in Central Asia, *Strategic Analysis*. xxiv(12):2273-2287.

Roy M. (2002). India-Kazakhstan: Emerging Ties, *Strategic Analysis*. 26(1): 48-64.

Roy M. (2008). 'Central Asia in the US Strategy: Changing Matrix'. *In:* Dash P. (eds.), *Emerging Asia in Focus: Issues and Problems*. Delhi: Academic Excellence, pp.209-233.

Roy M. (2010). 'Afghanistan and Regional Strategy: The India Factor'. *In:* Laruelle, Huchet F., Peyrouse S. and Balci B. (eds.), *China and India in Central Asia: A New Great Game*. UK: Palgrave Maclillan, pp. 61-80.

Rudenko Y. (2001). 'Indo-Kazakh Cooperation in Kazakhstan's Oil and Gas Sector'. *In:* K. Warikoo (eds.), *Central Asia and South Asia: Energy Cooperation and Transport Linkages*. New Delhi: Pentagon Press, pp. 86-97.

Sachdeva G. (2000). 'Joint Ventures and Export in the Caspian Sea Region'. *In:* Shamas-din (eds.), *Geopolitics and Energy Resources in Central Asia and Caspian Sea Region.* New Delhi: Lancer Books, pp. 120-132.

Sachdeva G. (2005). 'Central Asian Economic Transformation and Indian Response'. *In:* Rao N. and Alam M. (eds.), *Central Asia: Present Challenges and Future Prospects.* New Delhi: Knowledge World, pp. 283-300.

Sachdeva G. (2006). India's Attitude towards China's Growing Influence in Central Asia, *Central and Eurasia Forum Quarterly.* 4(3): 23-34.

Sachdeva G. (2007). 'Regional Economic Cooperation in Central Asia'. *In:* Santhanam, Baizakova and Dwivedi (eds.), *India-Kazakhstan Perspective: Regional and International Interactions.* New Delhi: Anamaya Publishers, pp. 111-124.

Sachdeva G. (2007). 'Tajikistan Economy and Indo-Tajik Trade and Economic Relations'. *In:* Santhanam K. and Dwivedi R. (eds.), *India-Tajikistan Cooperation: Perspective and Prospects.* New Delhi: Anamaya Publishers, pp. 98-117

Sachdeva G. (2010). 'The Reconstruction in Afghanistan: The Indian and Chinese Contribution'. *In:* Laruelle, Huchet, Peyrouse S. and Balci B. (eds.), *China and India in Central Asia: A New Great Game.* UK: Palgrave Maclillan, pp.173-195.

Sachdeva G. (2011). 'Indo-Central Asian Economic Relations'. *In:* Laruelle M. and Peyrouse S. (eds.), *Mapping Central Asia: Indian Perception and Strategies.* USA: Ashgate Publishing Company, pp. 123-141.

Sahoo P., Rai Kumar, Kumar R., (2009). *India-Korea Trade and Investment Relations*, Working Paper No. 242, Indian Council For Research on International Economic Relations (ICRIER), New Delhi.

Sakata Z. (2005). 'Russia and Central Asia: Problems of Security'. *In:* Rumer Boris (eds.), *Central Asia At The End of The Transition.* London: M.E. Sharpe, pp. 71-92.

Santhanam K. (2007). 'Enhancing India-Kazakhstan Science and Technology Cooperation'. *In:* Santhanam, Baizakova and Dwivedi (eds.), *India-Kazakhstan Perspective: Regional and International Interactions.* New Delhi Anamaya Publishers, pp. 64-70.

Sengupta D. (2005). 'India's Economic Presence in Central Asia: Prospects and Constraints'. *In:* Rao N. and Alam M. (eds.), *Central Asia: Present Challenges and Future Prospects.* New Delhi: Knowledge World, pp. 301-314.

Seznec F. (2000). 'Oil and Gas: Fuel for Caspian Economic Development'. *In:* Amirahmadi H. (eds.), *The Caspian Region at a Crossroad: Challenges of a New Frontier of Energy and Development.* London: Macmillan, pp. 105-120.

Sharma A. (2007). 'India's Investment in Tajikistan: Prospects and Challenges'. *In:* Santhanam K. and Dwivedi R. (eds.), *India-Tajikistan Cooperation: Perspective and Prospects.* New Delhi: Anamaya Publishers, pp.118-127.

Sharma Sen. (2010). *India and Central Asia: Redefining Energy and Trade Links.* New Delhi: Pentagon Press, pp.16-22.

Shen S. (2010). Great Power Politics: India's Absence from Ideological Energy Diplomacy in Central Asia, *China and Eurasia Forum Quarterly.* 8(1): 95-110.

Shepherd B. and Wilson J. (2006). *Road Infrastructure in Europe and Central Asia: Does Network Quality Affects Trade,* Research Working Paper No. 4104, The World Bank, Washington.

Shimomura Yasutami (1996). 'The Experience of Transitional Economies in East Asia: Implication for Central Asia'. *In:* Rumer Boris (eds.), *Central Asia in Transition: Dilemmas of Political and Economic Development.* London: M. E. Sharpe, pp. 237-272.

Sikri R. (2008). 'India's Relations with Central Asia'. *In:* Dash P. (eds.), *Emerging Asia in Focus: Issues and Problems.* Delhi: Academic Excellence, pp. 365-373.

Sikri R. (2009). India's Look East Policy, *Asia-Pacific Review.* 6(1): 131-145.

Singh A. (1995). India's Relations with Russia and Central, *International affairs.* 71(1): 69-81.

Singh K. (2010). India's Policy on Energy Security, in *India's Energy Security The Changing Dynamics.* New Delhi: Pentagon Energy Press, pp.15-50.

Sinitsina I. (2012). Economic Cooperation between Russia and Central Asian Countries: Trends and Outlook, Working Paper No. 5, *Institute of Public Policy and Administration*, University of Central Asia.

Smith A. (2009). 'Energy Governance: the Challenges of Sustainability'. *In:* Scrase I. and Mackerron G. (eds.), *Energy for the Future: A New Agenda.* England Palgrave Macmillan, pp. 54-74.

Starr S. (2005). *A Greater Central Asia Partnership for Afghanistan and Its Neighbors*, Central Asia-Caucasus Institute Silk Road Studies Program, March. Washington, D.C.

Stobdan P. (2009). India and Kazakhstan Should Share Complementary Objectives, *Strategic Analysis.* 33(1): 1-7.

Taneja N. Prakashm S. and Kalita P. (2013). *India's Role in Facilitating Trade under SAFTA*, Working Paper No. 263, Indian Council For Research on International Economic Relations (ICRIER), New Delhi.

Umarov K. (2004). Energy, Security, and Development: The Kazakh Experience, Contemporary Central Asia. 8(1-2): 1-16.

UNCTAD (2010): World Investment Report

UNCTAD (2011): World Investment Report

UNCTAD (2012): Handbook of Statistics

UNCTAD (2012): World Investment Report

UNCTAD: UNCOMTRADE Database

Volgina, Gafarly and Semenova (2001). 'The Transition to a Modern Market Economy'. *In:* Vassiliev A. (eds.), *Central Asia: Political and Economic challenges in the Post-Soviet Era.* London: Saqi Books, pp. 252-270.

Warikoo K. (2012). 'India and Central Asia: Potential Implication for Power Rivalries in Eurasia'. *In:* Shamas-din (eds.), *Geopolitics and Energy Resources in Central Asia and Caspian Sea Region.* New Delhi Lancer Books, pp. 98-116.

Weitz R. (2008). *Kazakhstan and the New International Politics of Eurasia,* Silk Road Paper, Central Asia-Caucasus Institute Silk Road Studies Program.

World Bank: WITS Database

World Bank: World Development Indicators (various issues)

World Trade Organisation: International Trade Statistics (various issues)

World Trade Organisation: World Tariff Profiles (various issues).

Yue C. (1999). Trade, foreign direct investment and economic development of Southeast Asia, *The Pacific Review.* 12(2): 249-270.

Zadeh P. (2000). 'The Geo-Politics of the Caspian Region'. *In:* Amirahmadi H. (eds.), *The Caspian Region at a Crossroad: Challenges of a New Frontier of Energy and Development.* London: Macmillan, pp. 175-186.

Zhukov S. (1996). 'Economic Development in the States of Central Asia'. *In:* Rumer B. (eds.), *Central Asia in Transition: Dilemmas of Political and Economic Development.* New York: M. E. Sharpe, pp.106-135.

APPENDICES

APPENDIX 1

Selected list of high level visits from India to Kazakhstan

Period	Visitor	Remarks
February 1992	P. Chidambaram, then minister of trade and commerce	The two countries agreed to accord each other the most favored nation treatment in all matters of trade and economic cooperation. Agreements were signed on the: a) diplomatic relations protocol to establish embassies and consultants. b) Cooperation in science and technology, culture and sports. c) Trade agreement. d) Banking agreement with state bank of India.
May 1993	Narshima Rao, then Prime Minister of India	Agreements signed included: a) agreement on technical cooperation between Kazakhstan and India. b) Cooperation in the field of science and technology. c) Credit agreement Kazakhstan and India. d) Agreement on establishment of joint inter governmental commission on trade commerce and scientific and technical cooperation. India also offered a credit line of $20 million to Kazakhstan.

June 1994	Salman Khursheed, Minister for commerce	Agreement to establish joint ventures and business council were signed. Also an agreement was signed to start a regular flights between Almaty and New Delhi
September 1996	K. R. Naraian, Vice President	High level meeting and cooperation agreements
September 1999	Jaswant Singh, Minister of External Affairs	Attainted CICA ministerial conference.
July 2005	K. Natwar, Minster of External Affairs	Attainted the SCO summit and India was admitted as an observer to the SCO.
February 2005	Minishanker Shanker Aiyer, Minster of Petrolium and Gas	Attainted the 5th meeting of the Kazakh-Indian inter governmental commission on trade, economics, S&T cooperation. MOU on cooperation between Kazmunaygaz and ONGC was signed.
April 2011	Manmohan Singh, Prime Minister of India	During this visit, several agreements were signed such as: a) agreement between ONGC Videsh Limited and Kazmunaigas on Satpayev Exploration Block. b) Agreement in cooperation in the peaceful uses of atomic energy. c) Joint Action Plan for furthering the Strategic Partnership between India and Kazakhstan (Road Map) for the period of 2011-2014. d) Agreement between the Ministry of Health of India and the Ministry of Health of the Republic of Kazakhstan on cooperation in the field of healthcare.

June 2011	S. M Krishna	Attend 10th summit of the SCO

Selected list of high level visits from Kazakhstan to India

Period	Visitor	Remarks
1992	Nursultan Nazarbyev, President	Declaration on main principles and directions of inter-state relations; protocol on establishment of diplomatic relations and agreements on cooperation in fields of trade and economic relations, S&T, culture, arts, education, mass media were signed.
February 1995	S.K Nurmagambetov, Minister of Defence	Issues pertaining to defence cooperation were signed.
March1999	Zh. Karibzhanov, Deputy Prime Minister	Attained an international conference entitled "Kazakhstan's investment opportunities" interacted with Indian business people.
2002	Nursultan Nazarbayev, President	In this visit both sides agreeing on foreign tie-ups in the a) oil and gas sector. b) Energy c) new technology (IT, Bio- and nano technology d) defence interaction e) trade and regional cooperation.
January 2003	Adilbek Zhaksybekov, Ministry of Industry and Trade.	A MOU on IT cooperation was signed.
November 2005	L. Kiinov, Vice-Minister for Energy and Mineral Resources	Attended International Round on Energy Cooperation, hosted by India's Minister for Petroleum and Natural Gas.

October 2006	Baktykozha Izmukhambetov, Minster of Energy and Mineral Resources	Attended 6th session of India-Kazakhstan Inter-Governmental Commission on trade, economic and science and technology cooperation.

APPENDIX 2

Selected list of high level visits from India to Kyrgyzstan

Date	Person	Remarks
Aug, 1999	Vice President, Krishan Kant	As chief Guest in the Kyrgyzs independence celebrations
2003	Prime Minster, Vajpayee	Signed a joint Declaration of friendship and cooperation Agreement on visa free regime for diplomatic passport holders, cooperation in the field of IT centre in Dushanbe were also signed
2007	Mr Murli Deora	Inaugurated the India-Kyrgyz Centre for Information Technology in Bishkek which was set up with Indian assistance.
Sept 2007	Mr O.P A rya	The 4th session of the India-Kyrgyz Inter-Governmental Commission on trade, economic, scientific and technological cooperation was held in Bishkek.
2011	Defence Minister, A K Antony	Inaugurated the India-Kyrgyz Mountain Bio-Medical Research Centre in Bishkek

Selected list of high level visits from Kyrgyzstan to India

Date	Person	Remarks
April 1999	Kyrgyzs President, Askar Akaev	An agreement on avoidance of double taxation, treaty on mutual legal assistance in criminal matters and a MOU on civil aviation matters were signed.
May, 2000	Mr Askar Aitmatov	Provided an opportunity for business communities of the two countries to directly interact with each other
Nov, 2003	President, Akaev	Participated in the UNESCO-sponsored "Education for All" This visit provides an opportunity to review bilateral relations and to discuss the regional situation.
2005	Kyrgyzs Defense Minister	Initiating dialogue for bilateral defense cooperation.
2007	Mr Adnan Karabaev	Review bilateral relations
2008	Minister of Foreign Affairs, Mr Adnan	Further review bilateral relations.
2010	Mr Kapar Kurmanaliev, Minister of Natural Resources	The 5th session inter-govt. commission on trade, Economic Scientific and Technological cooperation. A protocol was signed between the two countries for promotion of mutual investment in mineral exploration and development food processing etc.
Sept 2011	Defense Minster, Mr Abibila	Discussion on bilateral military cooperation, including defence research and development.

APPENDIX 3

Selected list of high level visits from India to Turkmenistan

April 2000	Foreign Minster, Mr. Boris Shikhmuradov	Discussion on bilateral and regional issues
Aug 2000	Minister of Culture, Mr. Oraz Aidogdiev	It was cultural troupe.
Nov 2005	Mr. A. K Pudakov, Head of Turkmenbash Oil Refinery and former Oil Minister of Turkmenistan	Attend conference of Asian Oil Ministers.
Oct 2006	E. Ahmad, Minister of State for External Affairs	1st meeting of the IGC was held, and discussed on issues of TAPI pipeline project.
December 2006	Prof Saifuddin Soz, Minster of Water Resources	Attendant funeral of Saparmurat Niyazov, President of Turkmenistan.
Nov 2007	Minister of Petroleum and Natural Gas, Mr. Murli Deora	Discussed with ministry of hydrocarbon resources about bilateral cooperation in the hydrocarbon sector

April 2008	Vice- President Shri Hamid Ansari	In the visit these countries signed MOU on cooperation in Oil and Gas sector.
Nov 2008	Minister of Petroleum and Natural Gas, Mr. Murli Deora	Review various business exchange, related with oil and gas, trade, IT sectors etc.
Sept 2009	External Affairs Minister Shri S M Krishna	Programme of Cooperation was signed between two foreign offices, discuss also on bilateral agreements between two countries and also visa policy relaxation. EAM handed over MoU to Turkmen, for the establishment of India-Turkmenistan Centre for Information Technology. The TAPI project was also discussed.
Feb 2010	Minster of State External Affairs Smt. Preneet Kaur	MoU was signed on establishment of an IT.
Oct 2011	Shri Sachin Pilot	Inaugurated IT Centre, Ashgabat University.

Selected list of high level visits from Turkmenistan to India

	Person	Remarks
Oct 2005	Vice- President Mr. Bairon Singh	Discussion with Turkmen Foreign Minster on Oil and Gas, Health and Education for bilateral cooperation, joint venture on Ajanta Pharma, Trilateral Transit Agreement.
January 2008	Deputy Prime Minster and Foreign Minster	Review the trade, economic, scientific and cultural relations between two economies.

| May 2010 | President Mr. Gurbanguly Berdimuhamedov | In this visit all, he met with President of India, Prime Minster and other Minster of the country. Six bilateral documents were concluded.a) Visa free for holders of diplomatic passport. b) education exchange programmes. C) agreement on trade and economic cooperation. D) agreement on cooperation in science & technology. e) cooperation in tourism, sports and media etc. f) MoU between FICCI and the chamber of commerce and industry of Turkmenistan. |

APPENDIX 4

Selected high level visits from India to Tajikistan

Date	Person	Remarks
Sept 2001	Minister of state for External Affairs, Mr Omar Abdullah	Anti-tuberculosis medicines worth Rs 20 lakh was gifted to Tajikistan
Nov 2003	Prime Minister, Vajpayee	This was first visit of PM of India to visit this country after independence of Tajikistan. In this visit President Rahmanov inaugurated India's Exhibition.
May 2003	Ministry of External Affairs	Establish Fruit Processing Plant in Capital of Tajikistan, funded by Indian government.
Jan 2003	Ministry of External Affairs, Mr Yashwant Sinha	Gifted a satellite dish antenna, colour Tv, and computer to Hindi Department (University of Tajikistan)
2005	Prime Minster, Vajpayee	Agreement on visa free for diplomatic passports.
2007	Minster of External Affairs, Mr N. Ravi	Reviewing the bilateral cooperation.
Oct 2007	Commerce Secretary G.K Pillai	Agreement on Double Avoidance of Taxation.

Aug 2008	Ministry of Petroleum and Natural Gas, Mr. Murli Deora	Discuss matters related bilateral and regional matters also inaugurated Varzob-1 hydroelectric plant.
Sept 2009	President Smt. Pratiba Devisingh Patil	This was first visit of state head to central Asia. She Iinaugurated the India-Tajikistan joint Business Forum.
Nov 2010	Minister of Power, Sushilkumar Shinde	Attend SCO meeting. Mr Shinde said that, India play a constructive role at the SCO platform for security and stability in the region.
May 2011	Shri P K Chaudhery, Special Secretary, Ministry of Commerce and Industry	The 6th joint commission between India-Tajikistan was held in Dushanbe.

Selected list of high level visits from Tajikistan to India

May 2001	President, Mr. Emomali Rakhmonov	The president of Tajikistan and Prime Minister of India discussed various international and regional issues and in this declaration India grant US$5 Million to Tajikistan. Fruit processing plant was sanction in Tjikistan.
Dec 2001	Defence Minister H.E Sherali Khairulloev	Review the situation of the region.
Oct 2003		Tajikistan open Embassy in India.
July 2006	Tajik delegation led Hakim Soliev, Minister of Economy.	Joint protocol for increasing economic cooperation between two countries was signed.

APPENDIX 5

Selected high level visits from India to Uzbekistan

Sept 2001	Minister of State for External Affairs, Mr Omer Abdullah	Handed over US$100,000 and anti-tuberculosis medicines to the Govt. of Uzbek as drought relief.
July 2001	Delegation from department of Customs	In this visit information on customs laws and regulations were exchanged and discussion on bilateral cooperation.
November 2003	Minister of External Affairs, Mr Yashwant Sinha.	An MoU was signed between Foreign Service Institute of India and Uzbek University of World Economy and Diplomacy.
April 2006	Prime Minister of India, Manmohan Singh	Set up inter governmental commission,
April 2007	Minister of State for Commerce, Jairam Ramesh	Chair the 7th session of India-Uzbek Inter Governmental Commission.
May 2007	Director of Entrepreneurship Development Institute of India, Divish Awasthi	Set up Entrepreneurship Development Centre in Uzbekistan.

September 2008	Minister of State for Commerce, Jairam Ramesh	The 8th session of India-Uzbekistan Inter Governmental Commission on trade, economics, scientific, technological and cultural cooperation.
October 2009	External Affairs Minister, S. M. Krishna	Signed an agreement to enhance economic relationship in health, IT and agriculture. India also gifted medical equipments and supplies worth US$ 1 million for hospital.
May 2010	Finance Minister, Pranab Mukherjee	Participate in 43rd meeting of the Asian Development Bank.
November 2011	Chief of Armay Staff, Gen V K Singh	Discuss defence cooperation between the two countries.

Selected list of high level visits from Uzbekistan to India

May 2000	Uzbek President H. E Islam Karimov	In this visit, both India-Uzbekistan signed eight agreements and provides an opportunity to exchange views on bilateral and regional issues.
February 2003	Uzbek Foreign Minster, Abdul Aziz	Signed an agreement for setting up a joint working group on International Terrorism
May 2003	Deputy Defense Minister of Uzbekistan	Signed a protocol for Defense cooperation.

2005	Uzbek President,	Signed agreement on cooperation in military and military-technical areas, culture, support of small and private enterprises and an exchange programme in the field of education. in addition signed eight documents in the fields of economy, commerce, education, tourism and culture etc.
September 2010	Chairperson of Uzbekistan Small Industries, llkham Khaydrov	Discusses matter related with mutual cooperation in the field of textiles.
May 2011	President Islam Karimov	Signed 34 documents/agreements